# Reading In

## Alice Munro's Archives

# Reading In

## Alice Munro's Archives

JoAnn McCaig

**Wilfrid Laurier University Press**

This book has been published with the help of a grant from the Humanities and Social Sciences Federation of Canada, using funds provided by the Social Sciences and Humanities Research Council of Canada. We acknowledge the support of the Canada Council for the Arts for our publishing program. We acknowledge the financial support of the Government of Canada through the Book Publishing Industry Development Program for our publishing activities.

## National Library of Canada Cataloguing in Publication Data

McCaig, JoAnn, 1953-
    Reading in : Alice Munro's archives


Includes bibliographical references and index.
ISBN 0-88920-336-9


    1. Munro, Alice, 1931-    .  2. Munro, Alice, 1931-    -Archives.   I. Title.


PS8576.U57Z76 2002              C813'.54                    C99-932372-5
PR9199.3.M8Z73 2002

© 2002 JoAnn McCaig


Cover art: *Between the Lines* (Party Series), mixed media
on paper by Gloria Kagawa, reproduced courtesy of the artist.
(View this and other works at http://www.gloriakagawa.com.)

Cover design by Leslie Macredie


The author and publisher have made every reasonable effort to obtain permission to reproduce the secondary material in this book. Any corrections or omissions brought to the attention of the Press will be incorporated in subsequent printings.

Printed in Canada

Dedicated

with affection and gratitude

to Helen Buss

and

to the Wednesday Circle:

Audrey Andrews
Donna Coates
Roberta Jackson
Elaine Park

# TABLE OF CONTENTS

# PREFACE

This is not the book I wanted to publish. This is not the book I originally wrote. The work before you is a drastically edited version of a manuscript (based on my doctoral research) which I submitted to Wilfrid Laurier University Press in the autumn of 1997. These changes became necessary when Alice Munro, along with her literary agent, Virginia Barber, and her editor at Knopf, Ann Close, declined to give me permission to quote from their correspondence, which is collected at the University of Calgary.

In the fall of 1997, Barber and Munro reluctantly granted me permission, through an intermediary, to quote their correspondence for an article in *Essays on Canadian Writing*. Ann Close queried a few items, but willingly gave her permission for the article, titled "Alice Munro's Agency: The Virginia Barber Correspondence." However, I ran into difficulty when I approached these three women directly in the spring of 1999 for permission to quote their letters in this book. In the cases of Close and Barber, there has been no direct refusal—simply no response. And initially, Munro only refused me permission to quote from her letters to John Metcalf, which are collected in his archive. At the time I thought, well, fair enough. These are per-

sonal letters sent to a friend and deposited, without Munro's
knowledge, in her friend's archive, which was then sold to a
repository. Munro never intended these letters to become public. The Salinger case, detailed in appendix 1, provides a guide-
post in this situation.

However, when John Metcalf quoted liberally from my *ECW*
article in a *National Post* essay in June of 2000 ("Canada's
Successful Writers Must Rely on Blessings from U.S. First" 17
June 2000: E4-5), his ideas (and mine) generated a strong reaction, including defensive responses from Robert Weaver's son
David, as well as writer Timothy Findley, editor Ellen Seligman,
publisher Douglas Gibson, and Alice Munro herself, who wrote
a letter to the *Post* speaking generously of Weaver and Metcalf,
but describing my article (the one extensively quoted by
Metcalf) as "riddled with bizarre assumptions and...written
with blatant disregard for fact" (Letters to the Editor, *National
Post* 29 June 2000). Shortly after this series of letters and articles in the *Post*—including my own response on 1 July, titled
"Obscure Canadian Essayist Responds"—I received a letter from
a lawyer writing on Munro's behalf, warning me that I did not
have permission to quote from Munro's unpublished letters or
her archive at all, either directly or in paraphrase form. Since
the book is a study of Munro's literary archive, this presented
me with a significant problem.

In order to obtain access to the Munro collection, I had indeed
signed forms in which I agreed not to publish material from the
archive without the consent of the copyright owner, namely the
author. But my thinking was, first, that the short excerpts I
intended to quote fell under the rubric of fair dealing or fair use.
Second, I reasoned that if permission were required for longer
excerpts, it would be granted. Munro and Barber had, after all,
given permission to quote for the *ECW* article, stating in a letter
to Robert Thacker, the editor of the issue, that though they grant
permission, "In doing so, we neither endorse nor dispute the
opinions or analysis of Ms. McCaig" (see note 10, chapter 1). I
therefore had reason to expect that a similar allowance would be
made when I published my research in a book. Third, I believed

(as did my publishers and academic advisors) that the availability of these documents to researchers implied that scholarly inquiry and publication were not only anticipated but welcomed.

A lengthy and rather confusing flurry of phone calls, faxes, and letters ensued, culminating in a comical interlude in which a scruffy academic like me finds herself in a lawyer's conference room in a splendiferous downtown office tower—the scruffy academic is dazzled by walls bedecked with the most glamorous contemporary Canadian art, and nearly blinded by the sheen of glass block, brass, and mahogany—while consulting with lawyers whose suits doubtless cost more than her monthly take as a postdoctoral research fellow.

The upshot was that, in the absence of permission to quote, I was forced to remove many pages of detailed discussion on the literary correspondence of Barber, Close, and Munro. In order to stay within the bounds of copyright law, large sections of my research are now given in summary form.

As I prepared this summary version for publication, a friend brought me galley proofs of a new book on Munro, *Lives of Mothers and Daughters,* written by the author's eldest child, Sheila Munro. Reading the reviews of this book has been intriguing for me. While opinions have ranged from positive to merely polite to derogatory, what nearly every review of Sheila Munro's memoir has in common is its listing of the things the critic has learned about Munro as a person. Charles Mandel at the *Calgary Herald* mentions the "revelations" that Munro "loathed Vancouver, had frequent panic attacks and had to see every movie Elizabeth Taylor was in" (7 April 2001: E7). *Quill and Quire* notes the following interesting "trivia: Alice's varicose veins and her few literary friendships" (April 2001: 26). In the *Globe and Mail,* Catherine Bush says that "some of the book's most revealing moments come not from its relatively uncomplicated emotional analysis but from small details: Alice, digging in the garden with a silver spoon, careless of decor and household furnishings, which mattered so much to Jim [Alice's husband] and Sheila; Alice, notable for her lack of physical dexterity, lifting her sunglasses from her eyes before crossing the street, 'as if she did not quite trust herself in the physical world'" (21 April 2001: D6). Bush also sensibly notes that "if…[the book] reads a little like an authorized biography, that's because it is." Sam Solecki comments, however, that "the book's few interesting parts deal with Alice Munro, though it doesn't reveal much we didn't already know from interviews, Catherine Sheldrick Ross's short 1992 biography *Alice Munro: A Double Life*, or the autobiographical stories" ("Still Growing Up," *National Post* 21 April 2001: B7). I must confess that I too was pleased to uncover certain bits of information that filled in an already fairly detailed picture for me. For example, I knew that, in the sixties, a University of Victoria professor's dismissive critique of Munro's stories nearly derailed her as a writer (see chapter 5), but I was intrigued when Sheila mentioned the man by name. He was one of my first creative writing professors, and a legendary curmudgeon. But what is the utility of this type of information, beyond personal interest, beyond gossip, beyond the cult of personality? What really intrigues me about Sheila Munro's "authorized" biography/memoir is that its existence indicates that Alice Munro is not averse to the publication of personal revelations, within limits, but that she appears to be averse to certain intellectual approaches to her life and work.

In the *Oxford English Dictionary*, "authority" is defined under two headings, both having to do with "power." The first definition relates to the power to enforce obedience. This type of authority, for my purposes, takes the form of the judges and institutions that enforce my obedience to the laws of copyright. It is the second aspect of the word "authority" which is more fruitful, however: "The power to influence action, opinion, belief." Several subheadings appear under this second definition, but the most useful are the last ones on the list: 8a: "The person whose opinion or testimony is accepted; the author of an accepted statement." 8b: "One whose opinion *on* or *upon* a subject is entitled to be accepted; an expert on any question." Munro's authority on the literary scene is the result of her exquisitely rendered short stories. Certainly, Munro's statements—fictional or otherwise—merit "widespread acceptance."

If I may lay claim to any authority in this matter, then mine would certainly be of the second type. In short, because of my research, I'm an authority on Alice Munro. An expert. (How terribly intoxicating, to claim authority. To claim power.) My expertise is the result of an immersion in traditional and contemporary theories of literature, culture, and authorship as a student, graduate student, and teacher of English literature, combined with nearly a decade of research on Munro's archive, as well as her published work, her biography, and pretty well every review, article, and interview that has appeared in the media since her career began.

However, readers who seek revelations about Munro's personal life will not find them in this book. No varicose veins, no Elizabeth Taylor movies, no silver spoons. This is not a biography of the woman but a study of the writer's career as it unfolds within a particular place and time, as revealed by archival documents sold by the author to the University of Calgary for purposes of scholarly research and study. The archival data had already been through two filtering processes by the time it came to me. First, the Munro collection was edited and selected by the author herself. Munro was very careful to include only documents pertaining to the business of writing; there are no personal letters or journals or diaries in the collection. The second filter was provided by the archival staff who catalogued the material. One library staff member I spoke to explained that the contract obliges the removal or restriction of any financial or extremely personal information unearthed in the cataloguing process. This librarian told me that, in the event that an excessively revealing personal document is found, the library staff will phone the author and ask, "Did you know that this was in here?" I have provided the final filter. Because my purpose is not an exposé of Munro nor of anyone associated with her, I have refrained from discussing certain documents overlooked by the author and the archivists.

What I originally wanted to do with Munro's archive was a project on her creative process as revealed in her story manuscripts. But when I began the PhD program, this initial idea was deemed too vague by the graduate committee, and my first two project proposals were refused. Academic institutions have in common with all cultural constructs a susceptibility to trends. I was summarily sent off to a remedial literary theory class and instructed to read Foucault.

I hated Foucault. I hated semiotics. I hated Lacan with a passion. Deconstruction baffled me. Finally, in a museum bookshop in Montreal, in the spring of 1995, I found a book called *The Field of Cultural Production.* The author, a sociologist named Pierre Bourdieu, appeared to be interested in the same sorts of impertinent questions I liked to ask about why literary culture is constructed the way it is.

It wasn't until a few months had passed, however, that Bourdieu's ideas began to mesh with my research. For I had found that I really couldn't do much with Munro's manuscripts—at least with what I knew then—because there were just too many, undated, handwritten, or manually typed. I couldn't make sense of them, beyond a close reading for textual variants—which was too traditional a project for the English department in which I was doing my graduate work. It was then that I turned my attention to a cultural analysis of the narrative of the author's career as I saw it unfolding in her correspondence files.

Cultural theory sometimes tends to make people uncomfortable, even angry. I once chaired a panel on Carol Shields at an academic conference and, when I made a comment about how closely Shields's work is tied to the sociohistorical real—for example to shopping malls and television—an audience member objected, "I don't see what TV commercials have to do with *Larry's Party*!" This person, like many, was fighting with all her might for the self-defining trope of high culture: Art is Art precisely because it is not Commerce.

Cultural theory certainly can unsettle and offend the well-developed sense of autonomy, of free will, of individualism, that is the foundation of Western thought. My own early forays into cultural theory felt like a personal assault, left me furious and resentful—how dare this professor or theorist suggest that I'm just some puppet being manipulated by invisible ideological forces, that my whole system of belief is a hallucinatory self-deception, that the world is really run by some decrepit little Wizard of Oz in a chintzy control booth?

Certain of the parties who have declined to grant me permission to quote from their correspondence have used words like "insulting" or "offensive" to describe my research. You would think that such reactions indicate that this book reveals all sorts of shocking personal information. It does not. What my book suggests is that Munro's writing career did not arise in isolation, but that, instead, various cultural, historical, and social factors played a significant role in the formation of her authorship. I suggest that Robert Weaver's mentorship was crucial to the establishment of Munro's reputation in Canada. I suggest that despite certain ideological tensions, the working relationship between Munro and her literary agent, Virginia Barber, has been important to her success. I suggest that the culture industry harbours a preference for the novel over short fiction, against which Munro has struggled and triumphed. I suggest that the public role of author is a source of ambivalence for Munro.

These are not particularly startling revelations—but what they suggest is that an author does not and cannot transcend culture but is instead enmeshed in it. As are all human subjects. Perhaps what some find so offensive in my work is merely the suggestion that art may not be the transcendant, self-perpetuating, autonomous structure that we need to believe it to be in order that we may call it art.

Perhaps it's true what Gloria Steinem said: "The truth will set you free, but first it will piss you off."

The way in which gender is implicated here must be acknowledged. To put it bluntly, the men said yes and the women said no. I sent permission requests to five men and three women. Four of the men returned the signed permission form promptly and without questioning my approach, my conclusions, or the exact nature of the quotation. (The fifth man was unable to respond due to illness.) The three women—Munro, Barber, and Close—declined to allow me to quote.

This is surprising to me, particularly as my approach is distinctly feminist, and if I were to be accused of ideological bias, it would certainly be pro-woman. It's a sad thought that, even in the twenty-first century, these three women who have achieved so much, who have reached such high ground and can claim such authority in their respective fields, would still feel it necessary to be so self-protective.

In the final analysis, it is true that Alice Munro has every right to supplement her writer's income by selling her papers to a university archive. It is also true that she has every right to construct and control her public persona to whatever degree she is able.

But it is problematic for me to think that repositories are spending public money to acquire literary archives, while their contractual arrangements with the authors create severe limitations on the academic freedom of inquiry of researchers. In short, if an author dislikes a scholar's methodology, analysis, or conclusions, then the researcher's freedom to publish his or her findings is severely compromised.

A work of extensive scholarship, if properly done, is a labour of love. It is conceived in a spirit of passionate admiration and interest, propelled by a profound intellectual and emotional engagement, and sustained in deepening understanding and respect. "Love" is not too strong a word to describe the impulse that inspires a scholar to devote many years of research to the work or life of an author. Despite the difficulties and countless revisions, despite my sense of "rejection" and "betrayal" in this "love" affair, I find that my admiration for Munro's work, and for the tenacity with which she struggled to produce it, remains undiminished. Likewise, despite the limitations under which this work is presented, my faith in the merit and the value of my analysis remains unshaken. What remains, I think, is a work which, though not true to my original conception of it, is still true to its own aims: to examine the way literary culture is constructed, and to set readers free to ask interesting questions of their own about literature, culture, and authorship.

# ACKNOWLEDGEMENTS

Thanks to Frank Davey for the good questions and to Robert Thacker for his invaluable Munro bibliography.

Thanks to the Special Collections staff at the Mackimmie Library for their assistance and many kindnesses.

Thanks and eternal admiration to Alice Munro for the great "material."

Thanks to Wilfrid Laurier University Press, particularly to former director Sandra Woolfrey and current director Brian Henderson for their unwavering faith in the value of this study, and to Barbara Tessman and Carroll Klein for their meticulous editing.

Thanks to Douglas Gibson, Charles McGrath, John Metcalf, and Robert Weaver for permission to quote from their correspondence.

## CHAPTER I

# INTRODUCTION

## Wrestling with a Fine Woman

November 22, 1971

Dear Alice Munro:

1) What kind of a childhood life did you *really* have (i.e. happy, sad, hard) and did you have any interesting experiences?
2) Why do you write? (i.e. release built-in tension, just for the fun of it)
3) Do you see yourself in the stories you write? (I see *myself* in your stories and I thought it probable *you* might).

(Munro Papers, MsC 37.2.55.7)

---

Notes for chapter 1 are on pp. 169-70.

## In Theory

In her introduction to the paperback edition of *Selected Stories,* Alice Munro describes the many letters she has received from readers over the years, asking questions like the ones listed above. For Munro, such inquiries are "rather flattering" because they "assume that I am a person of brisk intelligence, exercising steady control on a number of fronts" (ix). She then goes on to deconstruct the myth of herself as "brisk" and in "control," and instead points to the various factors, both mundane and intangible, that have made her the writer she is. On the mundane side, for example, she says that she writes short stories instead of novels partly because the demands of domestic life deprived her of the long periods of concentration needed for novel-writing, at least in the early years of her career. She implies that her later stories have "grown longer, and in a way more disjointed and demanding and peculiar" (x) partly because her children have grown up and left home. On the intangible side, Munro attempts to explain the almost mystical moment of recognition from which a story arises—an image, a moment, that demands the writer's attention—but for Munro, "these beginnings or essentials…are hard to explain and tend to fade anyway after the story has been put out in the world" (xiii). The closing paragraphs of the introduction are devoted to the process of revision, compared to which, Munro says, beginnings are "easy." She confesses that, as a young writer, she'd discard a story that wasn't working, but that "I am thrifty and tenacious now, no spendthrift and addict of fresh starts as in my youth" (xvi). The passive sentence construction in her description of the revision process is intriguing: Munro says "now that the story is free from my controlling hand a change in direction may occur" (xvi). Though often in the revision process she becomes "glum and preoccupied, trying to think of ways to fix the problem," she says that "Usually the right way pops up in the middle of this" (xvi). In both cases, the mundane and the almost mystical, there is a sense of the uncontrollability, the inexplicability, the fortuitousness of the creative process, almost as if Munro sees herself as a beggar maid fortunate enough to attract the beneficence of the kingly entity known as authorship, fortunate enough to be invited to sit at his feet. This self-construction, while typical of many literary authors, is somewhat belied by the evidence of the archive.

Like the anonymous fan whose letter is excerpted above, I have been curious for many years about Alice Munro, and like the letter-writer, I wonder how she *does* it. How has this truly exceptional writer achieved her enviable artistry and authority? In the course of answering this question, I also attempt to answer a larger one: How is authorship constructed in literary culture? My search for a method for answering these two questions leads to a third: How can literary archives—that is, the manuscripts, correspondence, and personal papers of authors— be used in conjunction with contemporary theories of literature to explain the inexplicability of authorship?

In the early stages of my research for a rather vaguely defined project "on" Munro's archives, I had occasion to read Audrey Thomas's story, "Initram," (which is the word "martini" spelled backwards). The story is narrated in the first person by a woman writer whose marriage is breaking up. This narrator goes to visit another woman writer, named Lydia, whose own marriage is also breaking up. Lydia "is" Alice Munro or, rather, she is a thinly fictionalized version of Alice Munro.[1] I was unsettled by "Initram"; I was almost offended by it. The story did things that stories are not supposed to do. First, it was autobiography masquerading as fiction—no, worse, it was *unauthorized biography* of Munro by her friend Thomas: in short, in addition to violating certain tenets of friendship, "Initram" violated the generic contract[2]—by which I mean the implicit agreement between author and reader about the form and content of the genre by which the work is classified, in this case a "short story." Second, it presented an author I held in high esteem in an unflattering light, violating the unfashionably humanist but nonetheless persistent view of the author as a uniquely gifted and admirable individual. Finally, it lied to *me*, violating the unspoken contract between author and reader that asks for the reader's willing suspension of disbelief in exchange for the pleasure of the (fictional, imaginative) text.

As I remarked my visceral reaction to "Initram," I began to ask what unacknowledged notions of authorship were giving rise to this sense of betrayal, of trespass. I decided that there must be some gap between theory and practice, between the ideal and the real—in short, between my theorizations of text and my actual consumption of it—between my scholarly training and my experience as reading subject. I suspected that this gap existed on the borderline between critical constructions of author, text, and reader and the actual practice of authorship, textuality, and reading in the sociohistorical present. I further suspected that the ideological contours of this gap might be legible in literary archives. Thus the questions raised by "Initram" presented me with the opportunity to use literary archives to study the notion of authorship as it exists not *inside* the lecture theatre or in scholarly criticism and theory, but in the *outside* world of markets, publishers, and readers. I would take my several and often conflicting notions of authorship and put them to the test of the literary archive of one Canadian woman short story writer, Alice Munro.

In the nineteenth and early twentieth centuries, compared to contemporary times, views of the author tended to situate authority in the person of the author him/herself, but recent theorists posit that the author function resides not in the personality of the author, but rather in his/her proprietary relationship with language. In *The Field of Cultural Production,* social theorist Pierre Bourdieu argues that "The true subject of the work of art is nothing other than the specifically artistic manner in which artists grasp the world, those infallible signs of his mastery of his art" (118). In 1968, Roland Barthes announced "The Death of the Author," and posited a "modern scriptor" whose "hand, cut off from any voice, borne by a pure gesture of inscription (and not of expression), traces a field without origin—or which, at least, has no other origin than language itself" (128). In Bourdieu's view, Barthes's ideas merely retain "the old tradition of internal reading so dear to the *lector academicus*" (178). For Bourdieu, Michel Foucault's is "the only rigorous formulation…of structuralism in relation to the analysis of cultural works" (178). In "What Is an Author?" Foucault says that "the fact that the discourse has an author's name, that one can say 'this was written by so-and-so' or 'so-and-so is its author,' shows that this discourse is not ordinary everyday speech that merely comes and goes, not something that is immediately consumable. On the contrary, it is a speech that must be received in a certain mode and that, in a given culture, must receive a certain status" (267). Like Barthes, however, Foucault locates what he calls "the author function" in language itself, arguing that the author's use of language is what gives the text its special status: "in a civilization like our own there are a certain number of discourses that are endowed with 'the author function,' while others are deprived of it. A private letter may have a signer—it does not have an author; a contract may well have a guarantor—it does not have an author. An anonymous text posted on a wall probably has a writer, but not an author" (267). Something that Foucault overlooks here, and which I will address throughout this study, is the irony that once the author function is in operation, all texts touched by the author's hand become imbued with authority; when an archive purchases Alice Munro's papers, it is not only her published texts that "receive a certain status" but also her letters, her contracts, her grocery lists.

An illustration of how the author function extends to unpublished materials, and how it posits a proprietary relationship with language, is found in Angie LeClercq's overview of how the Fair Use statutes in the United States apply to unpublished materials. (See Appendix 1.) LeClercq begins with the Copyright Revision Act of 1976, in which "an unpublished manuscript is protected by copyright from unauthorized use until fifty years after the death of the author" (109 ), thus according unpublished archival materials the same "authored" status as published work. Fair use is an exception to copyright, defined as "quotation or paraphrasing of limited portions of such unpublished documents without specific permission from the copyright holder for such purposes as news reporting, teaching, research and criticism" (109). LeClercq then goes on to describe a court case involving J.D. Salinger, wherein a biographer attempted to use seventy of Salinger's letters that had been deposited by the recipients' estates in various university archives. Salinger objected to this use of his "work" and won the case on appeal. The appeals judge ruled that while the recipient of the letter, and thereby the archive, "retains ownership of the tangible physical property of the letter" (116), the copyright owner retains his right to "the expressive content of the work, not the ideas or facts contained therein" (116). The judge ruled that the biographer had "no inherent right to copy the accuracy or the vividness of the letter writer's expression" (115-16). In short, the Salinger case shows how even the law locates the author function in language and the "accuracy" and "vividness" of its use; what belongs to the author is not *what* is said, but *how* it is said. In late capitalist culture, this proprietorship comes down to dollars and cents; thus Salinger's "right to control and potentially market a literary interest in unpublished primary materials" (116) was upheld.[3]

Foucault argues that, rather than reflecting culture and history, an author is constructed in culture and history; however, as several subsequent theorists have argued, some of the more practical and specific areas of culture and history are neglected in his theorization. In "What Was an Author?", her history of the legal notion of authorship, Molly Nesbit contends that Foucault's argument is weak on two points: the law and the market economy. First, detailing the evolution of French *droits d'auteur*, Nesbit asserts that the law "was only meant to distinguish a particular kind of labor from another, the cultural from the industrial" (249). This distinction bestowed a separateness or sanctity on the author, because the two qualities implied in the law are that cultural labour took place only in "the certified media"; and that "its privilege was justified by the presence of a human intelligence, imagination, and labor that were legible in the work, meaning that such work was seen...to contain the reflection of the author's personality" (249). Nesbit cites the exclusion of technical drawing from copyright laws as an illustration of the way in which the law attempts to distinguish culture from industry; technical drawing was excluded because "it had participated in the manufacture of industrial objects," and also because it "was *not* felt to reflect the personality of the draughtsman" (250). Second, according to Nesbit, "Modern culture existed as an economic distinction" (250), and the introduction of new technologies to the "certified media" began to raise the questions about authorship that engaged such thinkers as Mallarmé, Benjamin, Foucault, and Barthes. Nesbit says that the French copyright law and its subsequent modifications established that "the cultural was always being distinguished from its other, the industrial; culture's basic identity was always being derived from this distinction, which was always exceptional and always economic" (251). When such "authors" as photographers, filmmakers, and recording artists invaded the field in the twentieth century, however, "It was not so clear where one should be looking to find the reflection of the author's self" (254). Nesbit asserts that it is these economic and legal changes that raised the question of the author function, and that Foucault "neglected to explain that this [the author function] takes place within a market economy even though this economic condition...defined the author in the first place" (255-56).

Bourdieu takes a similar position. While he applauds Foucault's focus on "the primacy of relations" (*Field* 178), he also argues that Foucault does not go far enough. Like Nesbit, Bourdieu centers his objection on Foucault's failure to actively engage with the sociohistorical real; Bourdieu is doubtful about theories that "consider only the system of works, the network of relationships among texts, or intertextuality" (179) and are therefore "compelled to find in the system of texts itself the basis of its dynamics" (179-80). Likewise, for Bourdieu, "Exclusive attention to function...leads one to forget the groups that produce these objects" (181). Such groups belong to what Bourdieu defines as "fields"—"microcosms that have their own structures and their own laws" (181)—and he describes the literary field as "a space of objective relationships among positions—that of the consecrated artist and the *artiste maudit,* for example—and one can only understand what happens there if one locates each agent or each institution in its relationships with all the others" (181).

The Munro archive is a fruitful source of evidence of such relationships, and each of my chapters finds its touchstone in what Bourdieu describes as "the reintroduction of the specialists" (181) in which one may "apply a relational or...structural mode of thought to the social space of the producers" (181): I detail Munro's relational position in social space with such "specialists" as her mentor, Robert Weaver; her literary agent, Virginia Barber; editors such as Sherry Huber at Norton, Ann Close at Knopf, and Douglas Gibson at Macmillan and later McClelland and Stewart; and fellow Canadian writer John Metcalf. As Bourdieu points out: "The science of cultural works has as its object the correspondence between two homologous structures, the structure of the works (i.e. of genres, forms, and themes) and the structure of the literary field, a field of forces that is unavoidably a field of struggle" (183). It is precisely this "field of struggle" that my study illuminates, as I trace Munro's career from her earliest attempts to achieve publication to her present state of undisputed literary authority.[4]

Bourdieu's *The Field of Cultural Production* explores the parameters of the literary field, discussing the relationship between symbolic (or cultural) capital and economic capital. He points out the inverse relationship between these two concepts, the idea that commercial success diminishes the symbolic or cultural value of the work. Another important distinction is that between the field of restricted production (which is art for art's sake, or production for other producers) and the field of large-scale production (which is aimed at the general public). A third key concept is the idea of "disinterestedness," the cultural producer's disavowal of the economic. Bourdieu summarizes his argument as follows:

> The literary field is the economic world reversed; that is, the fundamental law of this specific universe, that of disinterestedness, which establishes a negative correlation between temporal (notably financial) success and properly artistic value, is the inverse of the law of economic exchange. The artistic field is a *universe of belief*. Cultural production distinguishes itself from the production of the

> most common objects in that it must produce not only the
> object in its materiality, but also the value of this object, that
> is the recognition of artistic legitimacy. (164)

Unlike Foucault, Bourdieu addresses in very specific terms the
market economy in which authors function. The way Bourdieu
grounds his study of cultural production in the sociohistorical
real makes his theories particularly useful to my discussion of
authorship and archive. In fact, my chapters will take up in turn
each of the descriptors of Munro enumerated earlier—
"Canadian" "woman," "short story" and "writer"—in order to
show the complex implications of seemingly simple terms when
they are viewed through contemporary theories of authorship,
as well as by the evidence of the archive.

   One aspect of inquiry that sets Bourdieu apart from other theorists of authorship is his recognition of the impact of social
class in the study of authorship and the cultural field. As Randal
Johnson comments: "The implication of Bourdieu's theory is
that any form of analysis which overlooks the social ground of
aesthetic taste tends to establish as universal aesthetic and cultural practices which are in fact products of privilege" (24).
Bourdieu himself describes "art and cultural consumption" as
"predisposed, consciously and deliberately or not, to fulfil a
social function of legitimating social differences" (25); however,
other areas of ideological tension appear to escape Bourdieu's
notice. He, like most of the author theorists, posits an author as
citizen of a major cultural power, such as France, Britain, or the
United States; as male; and as either a novelist, dramatist or
poet. For example, in Bourdieu's detailed study of the field of
cultural production, a glance at the index reveals no mention of
"feminist," "feminism," "gender," or "woman." Of the 219 names
listed in the index—names of writers, artists, and theorists—precisely four are names of women: playwright Françoise Dorin,
critic Julia Kristeva, and writers George Sand and Virginia Woolf.
No Canadians are named in the text or index. De Maupassant is
the only short story writer mentioned. In fact, in his discussion
of the economic and symbolic hierarchies of genre, Bourdieu
discusses only drama, poetry, and the novel. If contemporary

discussions of the author function centre on an author who is, for example, British, male, and a novelist, then how do such formulations of authorship apply to a Canadian woman short story writer like Alice Munro?

In "What Is an Author?" Foucault sets out four points that help me answer this question. He says that authorship is linked to institutions, that it is different at different times and in different civilizations, that it is defined not spontaneously but complexly and specifically, and finally that it does not refer to the individual but to the "plurality of selves" that defines the author function (271). My project is to identify specific institutions linked to Munro, such as academia, the literary marketplace, and cultural nationalism; to focus on a particular time (1950-99) and a particular civilization (Canada); to use archival materials to unravel at least some of the complexities and specificities of nationality, gender, and genre; and, finally, to theorize not the "real" Alice Munro, but the author function known as Alice Munro, a plurality of selves that combine to make her the Canadian woman short story writer described by American author Cynthia Ozick as "our Chekhov" and by the *Sunday Times* of London as "an unrivalled chronicler of human nature."[5] Despite the challenges she has faced as an author, Munro has reconfigured the cultural field. For example, a 1995 *Globe and Mail* review of a group of short story collections begins with the words: "To paraphrase Jane Austen, it is a truth universally acknowledged that a short story writer who wishes to be in possession of a good fortune must write like Alice Munro" (Harvey C7).

In examining the phenomenon of Munro's authorization as model short story writer, then, a question asked by Sean Burke goes to the heart of the matter: "Does the author reflect culture and history, or is the author constructed in culture and history?" ("Introduction" xv). I conclude that this is not an "either/or" question, and in the pages to follow, I discuss the ways in which Munro both reflects and is constructed in her own cultural milieu and her own historical moment.

For the purposes of this discussion, I ascribe neither to "the romantic notion of a writer's creative genius" nor to "an arti-

sanal view of authorship as analogous to any act of socio-economic production" (Burke, "Ideologies" 216); instead, I construct the author as a subject engaged in a lively, dynamic and
complex dialogue with her own sociohistorical situatedness, as
a "cultural worker" who both upholds and resists the status
quo, who exists in "a field of struggle...whose goal is the
preservation or transformation of the established power relationships in the field of production" (Bourdieu, *Field* 183). The
phrase "cultural worker" seems an appropriate starting point
for a study of "the science of cultural works" (183) in the sense
that I attempt to identify areas in which Munro transgresses or
transforms the field, such as the fields of nationality and
genre, and areas in which the struggles are somewhat less conclusive, such as the fields of gender, class, and the economics
of literary culture, fields in which "preservation" struggles
with "transformation." Conclusive or not, pyrrhic or not, the
struggles themselves are valuable for what they reveal about
the field. Detailing these struggles is also valuable in terms of
my own ethical agenda, since measuring the playing field is a
step toward levelling it. Bourdieu offers a similar rationale for
his approach:

> It is important, if one is to have a bit of freedom from the con-
> straints of the field, to attempt to explore the limits of the the-
> oretical box in which one is imprisoned. This, in my view, is
> the principal function of theoretical culture: to provide the
> means for knowing what one is doing and for freeing oneself
> from the naiveté associated with the lack of consciousness
> of one's bounds. (184)

In response to the concern that his approach is a means of
"reducing and destroying, in short breaking the spell of the
work" (190), Bourdieu counters with the assertion that "This
realistic vision, which transforms the production of the universal into a collective enterprise, subject to certain rules, appears
to me in the end more reassuring and, if I may say so, more
human than the belief in the charismatic virtues of pure interest
in pure form" (191). I agree with Bourdieu that putting a more

"human" face, and a more sociohistorically situated aspect, on authorship is a worthwhile and necessary "disenchantment" (Bourdieu 130).

Cultural studies is broadly defined by Simon During as "the study of contemporary culture," an approach that has been developing since the 1950s and that, ironically, finds its genesis in Leavis's concept of the dissemination of the Great Tradition as a means of morally improving the masses. In the "culturalist" branch of the discipline, influenced by theorists such as Bourdieu and Foucault, critical attention is focused on the economics, politics, and history surrounding the literary work, and on the concept of "fields" (the various institutions which structure our lives). This concept, which acknowledges humans as subjects in ideology, also sees various fields as containing "choices of 'self-formation,' or what Foucault called 'self-government'" (During 11), or what Paul Smith would call "agency" (xxxv). The concept of "self-government" is evident in Foucault's remarks on the misconception of power as mere "repression" or "subjugation." Instead, he asserts that "individuals...are always in the position of simultaneously undergoing and exercising... power. They are not only its inert or consenting target; they are also the elements of its articulation" ("Two" 98). Paul Smith, in *Discerning the Subject*, takes a similar position on human subjectivity: he uses the term "subject" as "the conglomeration of *positions*, subject-positions...into which a person is called momentarily by the discourses and the world that he/she inhabits," whereas the term "agent" describes "a form of subjectivity where, by virtue of the contradictions and disturbances in and among subject-positions, the possibility (indeed, the actuality) of resistance to ideological pressure is allowed for" (xxxv). In short, despite the fact that humans are subjects in ideology, areas of choice, self-formation, resistance, and agency are available.

The pertinence of such notions to this study of Munro's authorship can be illustrated by two brief examples: First, when I examine different versions of an early Munro story, called "Goodbye Myra" in *Chatelaine* in 1957 and retitled "Day of the Butterfly" in her first book in 1968, my discussion of the textual alterations the author made does not focus on how the story or its author had "matured" or how the changes made the story "better." Instead, I am interested in how these edits and emendations speak of Munro's agency in choosing to move from the popular field to the literary field (or what Bourdieu describes as "the field of restricted production"), and what these specific changes to the text indicate about the ideological contours of late twentieth century fiction. Similarly, in my second example, cultural factors inform my approach to a letter to Munro from American literary agent Virginia Barber. On the back of the letter is a telephone doodle, in which the name Alice Fremlin is written twice, as is the name Alice Munro, as is the name of Munro's lover and soon-to-be second husband, Gerald Fremlin.[6] Seeing the power of the author function juxtaposed with the subjection of romantic dreaminess leads me to speculate that a tension exists between the subject positions of "author" and "woman."

My primary source is the Alice Munro fonds, a collection of personal papers and manuscripts housed in Special Collections at the Mackimmie Library at the University of Calgary. Though my discussion is informed by my reading of Munro's published books, this study does not attempt to analyze her literary work. Such analysis has been done in such admirable studies as Ajay Heble's *The Tumble of Reason,* Magdalene Redekop's *Mothers and Other Clowns,* Beverly Rasporich's *Dance of the Sexes,* and James Carscallen's *The Other Country,* to name a few recent examples. It is my conviction that literary archives are an underutilized source of useful information about culture, authorship, and literary process. I therefore concentrate my discussion on archival evidence, and refer to published and collected work only when indicated by the argument.[7]

Particular attention is given to materials from Munro's midcareer, since the seventies are a particularly intense and fascinating period in her authorial history. It is during this time that she enters the American literary marketplace, marries for the second time, and struggles with genre privilege while preparing *Who Do You Think You Are?* for publication. In general, the tensions between nationality, gender, and genre all clash during this period, and some very powerful negotiations are needed to bring Munro into the full force of her own authority.

In a 1944 article called "Reflections of an Archivist," Sir Hilary Jenkinson uses the language of religion to describe his area of study; Jenkinson says that "the sanctity of evidence" is "the Archivists' creed" (21). He adds that the archive is "an evidence which cannot lie to us...*provided that it has come to us in exactly the state in which its creators left it*" (20). Such a proviso is problematic, when I consider that if the Alice Munro archive had come to me exactly as its creator left it, I would be pawing through the jumbled contents of a steamer trunk and a battered blue suitcase. Instead, the evidence before me is catalogued, organized, and edited not only by its creator, Alice Munro, but also by the archivists who received it—archivists who decided, for example, that letters from editors, publishers, and peers should be assigned to individual files, while letters from ordinary readers should be collected in a single folder. Whereas Jenkinson's approach might be labelled traditional, the influence of contemporary theory is evident in Brien Brothman's 1991 article "Orders of Value: Probing the Theoretical Terms of Archival Practice," in which he warns archivists against thinking that they and their work "transcend culture" (91). Instead, Brothman suggests that inclusion, exclusion, and arrangement are based on socially determined concepts of value. According to Brothman, the "Jenkinsonian sense of personal abstention— a requirement of self-effacement" in archivists is both blind and dishonest, for archivists are not simply "acquiring" and "preserving" records, they are "creating value" (82). An illustration of this occurs in a *Saturday Night* article by Martin Knelman, in which Alice Munro discusses the sale of her papers to the University of Calgary, and says, with astonishment and delight, "They'll take *anything!*" (18). I recounted this comment to Special Collections librarian Apollonia Steele, who replied with equal delight, "Authors don't realize the value of their materials." Steele's reaction indirectly subscribes to the view that archivists do build and construct, at least to the degree that they value items the author disregards. The economic implications of this creation of value cannot be overlooked. It has been said that, for many Canadian authors, the sale of papers to an archive can generate more income than the proceeds from their published works.

I agree with Brothman that words like "true," "faithful," "integrity," "impartiality," and "guaranteed trustworthy" (as used by archival theorists such as Jenkinson and Terry Eastwood) cannot be used unproblematically in reference to archives, any more than words like "intention," "meaning," and "author" can be used unproblematically in discussions of literary texts. In "The Archive as a Literary Genre: Some Theoretical Speculations," Pamela Banting describes the archive as "an avant-garde literary mode that deconstructs traditional ideas of the book and the author"; for Banting, the archive is interesting both for its "creative, subversive powers" and for its "support of, and participation in, the existing structures of power and authority" (119).

Like Banting, I find the archive a site of creativity; I enjoy my hours there, playing cultural studies sleuth, literary detective. "Aha!" I say to myself. "Yes!" I scrawl in the margins of my notebook. And, to my embarrassment, I occasionally shout "Wow!" into the silent, rarefied air of the Special Collections Reading Room, startling my more dignified colleagues. I am playing with the archive, extracting its open secrets—or wait a minute, is the archive playing with me? I am making it produce interesting information, I am extracting data, but at the same time the author and archivist through their omissions, restrictions, and selections manipulate me. Why is this letter in duplicate? Why is this file restricted? Why are certain letters referred to in other documents absent from the archive? Am I the butt of an authorial joke (a la Richler, Byatt, Shields, Lodge)[8] on earnest, trivia-obsessed researchers? Am I being led around by the nose? Or worse, by the ego?

In April 1995, when I was about halfway through the writing of this study, I had occasion to meet Alice Munro in person. I introduced myself, and described my research. "Oh my God," she said, laughing, "you know *everything*!" I wanted to protest that, despite countless hours in the archive, I often feel that I know nothing at all, but instead I laughed with her, understanding then as now that what I know is a mere fraction of "everything." But it is an important, interesting, and revealing portion of the story—not *the* truth, but *a* truth about the author function—the "plurality of selves"—known as Alice Munro.

In accepting my ambivalent place as "worker" of and in the archive I realize that my own position as a human subject guides my research. Maurice Biriotti articulates the dilemma in his observation that, for the critic, "dealing with the author presents a number of complex problems. But these problems are compounded by the fact that the critic also writes, is also an author, is also implicated in the very structures of authority about which he or she writes" (13). Biriotti thus raises the problematic question of authorial objectivity, and his point is a good one. While I may claim to have researched the theory, the published work, and the archive, I also recognize that I speak from a specific sociohistorical context, and that my account is therefore coloured by my own subjectivity as a white female academic, a single mom, child of the sixties, and product of a privileged upbringing. Thus I can make no claim to unqualified objectivity.

What I *can* do, however, in taking a cultural studies approach to Munro's archive and authorship, is to look askance at the way things are, at what is "natural," at what is described as "common sense." Cultural studies functions by looking at the sociohistorical roots of common-sense assumptions about the nature of reality and by finding those roots in the systems that organize our lives, such as patriarchy, capitalism, rationalism, Aristotelian philosophy, and religious dogma. The point is to suggest that systems of belief are just that: sociohistorically grounded collective hallucinations that can be questioned, that can be dispelled, that can be changed. The opportunity to do this type of academic research has provided me with a vocabulary and a forum for my innate rebelliousness, as well as the chance to "break the spell of the work" (Bourdieu, *Field* 190) and thus achieve a more "human" perspective on the cultural field.

This is a relatively new way to approach literary archives, which, in the past, appear to have been used mainly to write literary history, to trace the development of image patterns, or to explicate and further elevate the published text. It seems to me that there is an untapped potential in literary archives, and that cultural studies theory can be usefully applied to all types of texts, published or not.

However, the theorists whose work forms the theoretical underpinnings of this study usually work from male examples. As noted, Bourdieu names few women in his lengthy study of the field of cultural production; Foucault names only one woman in his discussion of authorship; in "The Writer on Holiday," Barthes describes "the Writer" as "he" and "him," as a person who might have "a liking for 'pretty girls, *reblochon* cheese and lavender-honey'" (33). In *The Scholar Adventurers*, Richard Altick examines the attractions of scholarly curiosity, quoting a seventeenth-century marquis as saying that research "hath a pleasure in it like that of Wrestling with a fine Woman" (15). And, in his detailed and meticulous work called *Principles of Textual Criticism*, James Thorpe comments on how "the intentions of the person we call the author...become entangled with the intentions of all the others who have a stake in the outcome, which is the work of art" (30); yet he implies that some of those who "have a stake in the outcome" are less qualified than others to interfere when he says that "I suppose almost every writer—even the lowly scholar—has found his deathless prose altered by a publisher's editor, who is sometimes an eminent man of letters and sometimes a mere slip of a girl barely out of college" (18).

Given the relegation of females to inferior status in the very theoretical works that generate my approach, one of the biggest challenges for me in the production of this study has been granting the author function to myself, to find my own way, given my gender, of "Wrestling" with that "fine Woman," the archive. I am, after all, not an eminent man of letters, but a mere slip of a girl barely out of college. Like my subject, Alice Munro, I have had to wrestle with the lies, secrets, and silence[9] that are my cultural inheritance, and have had to grant myself the authority to speak.

At the same time, I recognize that, like my subject, my self-construction is always prey to my unconscious subjection to cultural ideology and to the vicissitudes of the sociohistorical. The real "beggar maid" in this study is not Alice Munro, but me.

## In Practice

That said, reading into archival records nonetheless presents certain practical problems. This I learned when attempting to obtain permission to quote passages from the various documents cited in this book and encountering resistance from some of the parties involved. The tension between theory and practice tends to manifest itself in three different forms:

1. memory, that slippery and mysterious human instrument
2. context, as in absence of or lack of access to
3. self-construction, as a factor in reading and interpretation.

### 1. Memory

When I originally wrote to Munro's editor at Knopf, Ann Close, to request permission to quote from her correspondence with the author, she asked to see text and context. I replied with the text of the two paragraphs of Close's correspondence, and with the text of a footnote which explicates a reference in one of the letters. Two assertions in the footnote were questioned by Close, but when I provided documentary evidence from the archive for my assertions, she admitted that she had forgotten she'd said or done these things and agreed to allow me to quote her for the purposes of the article in *Essays on Canadian Writing*. Unfortunately, Close has not responded to my requests for permission to quote her correspondence with Munro for this book. (See preface).

In this case, the technical difficulty was primarily related to memory. Close objected to an assertion but responded favourably when presented with documentary evidence that she had indeed said these things. Few of us remember everything we say and do in the course of a day, particularly as time goes by.

## 2. Context

Say, for example, that in the thick of my discussion of the very problematic publication history of *Who Do You Think You Are?*, I note several things. I note intense pressure from Munro's then-publisher, Norton, to transform the linked short story collection into a novel. I also note a six-month gap in Munro's correspondence from Virginia Barber. This leaves me wondering where Barber stands in the debate—whose side is she on? A Barber letter which breaks this gap, a letter which I am unable to quote, might lead me to speculate that Barber is trying to convince Munro to transform her story collection into a novel. Because of my *reading in* of the present state of affairs with the forthcoming book, I interpret certain phrases in Barber's letter as a reference to the story which will tie the collection together. The notion of tying the book together somehow is certainly on Barber's mind, as a letter of June 20 indicates in its reference to how Anne Tyler cobbled a group of short stories together in a recent novel, a copy of which Barber is forwarding to Munro (MsC 38.2.63.12).

Furthermore, I read Barber's tone in this letter as an indication of the tension present at this point in their association; she seems rather dismissive, not at all like the enthusiastic recipient of previous Munro stories (MsC 38.2.63.2). A mention of Barber's then five-year-old daughter, Jenny, is cryptic, but on the whole, this seems a reasonable enough reading.

But here, the archive misleads. In subsequent correspondence from Munro and Barber, I discovered that the phrase in question refers to an incident which occurred when Munro and Barber were walking Jenny to preschool. Munro attempted to use this incident in her fiction but ultimately found that the material did not work and dropped it. I further discovered that what I understood as the dismissive tone in the letter was nothing of the kind, according to Barber, who merely delays a full reading of her authors' new work for times when she is away from the office, and can luxuriate in the work undisturbed, at home.[10] (One of the editors of this volume concurs, saying that a "glance" can be an indication of a reader's eager anticipation of the pleasure of a full reading in more leisurely circumstances. However I, as writer, am probably particularly sensitive to the notion of a "glance". When my work arrives on the desk of one who has the power to market it, I want nothing less than choirs of angels ascending with trumpets blaring, then a heavenly white light to bathe the reader in silent awe.... I further suspect that I am not the only writer who desires such rapt attention.)

The problem is available context. In an essay called "The Colonel's Hash Revisited," Munro questions a critic who interprets her story in a way antithetical to her own vision of her creation.[11] Yet she acknowledges that, once a story has gone out in to the world, the author must resign herself to such misreading. And must accept it—just as I must accept readers' judgements and (mis?)readings of *this* work. However, an archival reading risks a like offense, in constructing not a critical interpretation of a literary text, but of a culturally contextualized career.

Yet, if archives pose such risks, are so deficient in context, so blind to nuance, so prey to tricks of memory and monoliths of self-construction, then how are they to be used at all? Certainly, the archive comes with contextual limitations. It is only what it is—a collection of inanimate objects whose content paints a picture without access to certain shadings of, say, friendship, nuance, shared jokes, history. Yet, if we accept that a literary work must be read *as is,* then we have accepted the fact that we cannot have the author standing at our shoulder, explicating the text, filling in the gaps, saying "What I meant here was...". Rather, the work must stand on its own. The archive must be read the same way. The fact of the archive is that, like a published work, a) its availability to readers and researchers is an indication of its cultural value, b) it has an economic value which accrues to the author, and c) it offers certain aesthetic/informational value. In this sense, the archive may be thought of as a literary text, and may (must) be read with same closeness, analytical acuity and interpretive skill as any Munro short story. Though the archive contains "unpublished materials," the fact that it is accessible to the public makes it a published text in the sense that it is available for scrutiny by readers. Thus, like the roofed-over cellar in Munro's story which is, in her view, misinterpreted as a symbol for death and burial, the archive is no longer an innocent object.

## 3. Self-Construction

My previous point about my own writerly desire—to be appreciated, acknowledged, treasured—ties into the thorny problem of self-construction, as in fact does the Ann Close discussion. The human subject constructs itself according to a complex system of beliefs, bringing these beliefs to every act, every statement, every analytical process. An added dimension is the self-consciousness of the archival document. Once a writing subject becomes aware of her potential reading public, this awareness inevitably colours the constructed self. For example, in a letter of 29 January 1980, Barber jokes that a recent amusing letter from Munro will no doubt please some graduate researcher in the year 2000 (MsC 38.2.63.41). Negotiations for the purchase of the Munro papers by the University of Calgary are first mentioned in the Barber correspondence in January 1979. Truer words were never spoken, as now, in the early twenty-first century, this (former) graduate student has been immensely cheered (but also challenged) by the documents which Munro has made available to researchers.

When I interpret the correspondence between, say, an author and her agent, three unique and largely irreconcilable organizations of subjectivity come into play. There's the literary author, part of whose authority is formed on her "disavowal of the economic"—in brief, she is an artist, not a hack. There's the literary agent, who finds herself at the uncomfortable cultural juncture where art meets commerce; her job is to make the work of art marketable while at the same time preserving the integrity of the artist she represents. Finally, there's the archival reader and literary critic, privileging the aesthetic over the industrial, the artist over the business person—an occupational hazard of one whose professional life is devoted to the study and teaching of literature.

Say then that I, the academic reader, encounter letters which, to me, quite pointedly highlight the class or economic gap between author and agent. A reader whose position is defined by her awareness of class, as well as her position of "defender of the faith" in terms of "her" author, might read these letters with a jaundiced eye. Perhaps she'd be struck by a sense of injustice that a Canadian woman short story author of four books, and winner of two Governor-General's awards, and holder of a first refusal contract with the *New Yorker* still struggles financially while her American "cultural banker" (Bourdieu 75) lives the good life, no doubt with the help of her ten to twenty percent cut of Munro's earnings.

Yes, that is one reading.

Here's another: What if the Barber/Munro agent/author relationship in fact contains no trace of class distinction or inequity, and is merely a successful partnership enriched by warm friendship? What if my reading overlooks the fact that I probably would not be reading these letters if Munro had lacked the support of a savvy agent to market her archive to the University of Calgary?

In effect, *any* discussion of class position, privilege, inequity is fraught with potential insult to the necessary mis-recognitions on which self-constructions, and the construction of relationships, are founded. Munro's own acute aware-ness of this is clear in her story "Rich as Stink," in which a young girl, Karin, hears the title phrase used to describe her own mother: "Karin felt her face heat up, she felt the shock of those words. It was something she'd never heard before. *Rich as stink.* It sounded hateful" (*Love of* 237). The hatefulness is compounded by two facts: the speaker who describes Karin's mother as "rich as stink" is the mother's former lover, and he says this while urging Karin to stay on her mother's "good side" in order, presumably, to profit from her mother's wealth. For Derek to speak of the mother/child relationship in mercenary terms is hateful indeed, particularly because of Karin's dependence in this relationship, one which is not of her own choosing.

A "rich as stink" reading of Barber's letters risks the same hatefulness, the same shock, the same assault on a relationship of interdependence, a relationship which functions very successfully on intertwined recognitions and misrecognitions. Whatever the economic facts of the author/agent relationship, however submerged, disavowed, or simply unproblematic, the salient point is that Barber and Munro are friends as well as business partners—a binary that is crucial to their mutual success. Just as the "disavowal of the economic" is crucial to the self-construction of the literary author, so the same disavowal is crucial to warm, supportive relationship between author and agent, which allows them to transcend the dictates of literary culture.

Thus, while I may "read in" to the Munro archive with all my biases in play, I also pay due respect to questions of memory, context and self-construction, particularly as they bespeak the interplay of recognition and misrecognition that is crucial to the creation of Alice Munro as Canadian Woman Short Story Writer.

## CHAPTER II

# "CANADIAN"

## Creating the Creator

November 5, 1968


Munro's Bookstore
753 Yates Street


Dear Alice:

I was glad to see you again and sorry that I missed Jim. I hope he has recovered from his trip. Now that you have begun to write some new stories once more, I hope you will keep at it and can I encourage you soon to give me one for *Anthology*. With the hour I now have, I really am in a better position to go looking for new material and I'd love to have a story of yours sometime this winter if that seems at all possible.
Yours sincerely,
Bob
Robert Weaver

(MsC 37.2.8.9)

---

Notes for chapter 2 are on pp. 170-73.

In a discussion titled "Who Creates the Creator?," Bourdieu asks "Who is the true producer of the value of the work—the painter or the dealer, the writer or the publisher?" (*Field*, 76). He remarks on how "the ideology of creation...makes the author the first and last source of the value of his work," thus concealing the importance of the "cultural businessman" in the production of symbolic value (76). The archival correspondence between Robert Weaver and Alice Munro covers a period of more than twenty years and describes a mentoring relationship crucial to Munro's establishment of literary authority in Canada. In addition to his production work at CBC, Weaver was a founding editor of the *Tamarack Review* and also functioned as editor of many collections of Canadian short fiction (see Appendix 2). Sandy Stewart, in his history of Canadian radio, describes Weaver as "the godfather of Canadian writing," and adds, "Almost every successful contemporary writer in Canada has benefited from Weaver's guidance and encouragement" (155). Bronwyn Drainie concurs, saying that from the mid-fifties to the mid-sixties:

> it's only the mildest form of Canadian exaggeration to say that Robert Weaver, through his twin outlets, CBC radio and *Tamarack Review*, kept fiction writing alive in this country. His great discoveries were Mordecai Richler and Alice Munro, but virtually every substantial fiction writer in Canada benefited from Weaver's understated and tireless devotion to the development of Canadian literature. (289-90)

The history of the expansion and cultural aims of the CBC put Robert Weaver in a unique position to help Canadian writers like Munro. Weaver joined the Talks and Public Affairs Department of the Canadian Broadcasting Corporation in 1948, and worked for the CBC until his retirement in 1985. He was hired to work on *CBC Wednesday Night*, an "imaginative experiment" that "quickly became a unique institution in this country, and the three hours a week of cultural entertainment provided an important outlet for the work of Canadian poets, authors, and playwrights" (Weir 275). Weaver created the radio program *Anthology*, a "weekly thirty-minute series with a modest budget," which was broadcast on the AM network of the CBC at Weaver's insistence, as he wanted to reach the broadest audience possible. In 1969, *Anthology* moved to Saturday night and was lengthened to an hour. The program included "poetry and short story readings, talks, interviews and discussion, features and documentaries," and Weaver notes proudly that "most of the material broadcast on *Anthology* has been by Canadian writers and performers, but we have tried not to ignore the rest of the world even during that period when cultural nationalism was fashionable in this country" (xi-xii). As a salaried employee of a government institution, Weaver had little to gain financially from the success or failure of his proteges, yet he was an important mediator between the individual and culture.

Outside the confines of the CBC, Weaver was also an important historical figure in the marketing and promotion of Canadian literature, short fiction in particular. In addition to founding and editing the *Tamarack Review*, he was also a well-known anthologist of Canadian short stories.[1] In 1952, just four years after he joined the CBC, Weaver edited, with Helen James, an anthology called *Canadian Short Stories*, for Oxford University Press. He was then invited to take over the editorship of a series for Oxford, and further collections appeared in 1960, 1968, 1978, 1985, and 1991. As Weaver notes in his Preface to the 1991 edition, "only two writers have appeared in all five of these anthologies: Mavis Gallant and Alice Munro" (*Canadian*, 5th Series, xi).

In a country where short story anthologies were few and far between, Weaver's power in both the broadcast and print media was significant, and writers such as John Metcalf have tended to question the way in which both Weaver's media and his personal tastes affected literary production. Using the short fiction of Norman Levine as an example of how the medium of radio could affect writing, Metcalf observes: "Norman Levine depended on Weaver to keep him alive and this forced him into a kind of writing for radio. When he was no longer writing for radio, his stories got longer, deeper, more exploratory, more fragmented" (qtd. in V. Ross A10). Metcalf adds that "It would be possible to say that Weaver has promoted the conservative, the rural, the realistic—writing with quiet, solid good taste over the fantastic and the imaginative"; however, Metcalf concedes that, "In most cases he's been very tolerant" (A10).

Munro herself disagrees with Metcalf's accusation of conservative bias: Weaver, she claims, "never limited his interest to any one kind of writing, to any particular kind of material or set of preoccupations. He understands the breadth and diversity we need to have a literature" (Foreword x). This is probably the closest Munro ever comes to making a statement on "CanLit," and it also betrays what is perhaps her strongest objection to cultural nationalism: that its striving for unity and national identity stifles literary breadth and diversity. However, a glance at the tables of contents of anthologies edited by Weaver tends to bear out Metcalf's criticism. Though the collections do make room for works by experimental writers such as Dave Godfrey, David Helwig, or Audrey Thomas, and for marginalized voices like those of Dionne Brand, Neil Bissoondath, and Daniel David Moses, on the whole the Weaver collections tend more toward the mainstream than those edited by Metcalf himself, or the *New Canadian Stories* editions of Clark Blaise. Furthermore, what Metcalf says of Levine is also true of Munro: her mature stories have become "longer, deeper, more exploratory, more fragmented" than the work she sold to *Anthology*—though this shift could just as easily be attributed to the gradual easing of her domestic responsibilities as well as to the fact that, as her consecration as a serious artist is more firmly established, she is able to allow herself more stylistic experimentation and risk-taking. Whether or not Weaver is guilty of a realist bias, his aesthetic and Munro's were a good fit, at least in her "formative" years.

In his discussion of relations between writers and publishers, Pierre Bourdieu describes publishers as "equivocal figures" who "need to possess, simultaneously, economic dispositions which, in some sectors of the field, are totally alien to the producers and also properties close to those of the producers whose work they valorize and exploit" (*Field* 39). Considering how, in general, most writers regard cultural power brokers and bureaucrats with the most profound suspicion, Robert Weaver has managed his equivocal position masterfully, for he is surprisingly well respected in the Canadian writing community. Hugh Garner once dedicated a volume of his stories as follows: "To Robert Weaver, broadcaster and editor, who has done more for the modern Canadian short story than anyone else in this country." Hugh Hood calls him "The most astute talent-spotter in the history of English-Canadian literature." To playwright Len Peterson, Weaver is "a kind of cross between a cultural one-man Salvation Army and a soup-kitchen Canada Council," while George Woodcock observes: "It was he who nurtured the short story over the past quarter of a century in Canada, when magazine editors were growingly disinclined to publish fiction; he did so by a judicious use of CBC patronage and by persuading often resistant publishers to bring out a series of short story anthologies under his editorship."[2] Al Purdy says, "His importance is whatever importance you attach to writing itself" (V. Ross A9). In her Foreword to *The* Anthology *Anthology,* Munro credits Weaver with "giving us [i.e., writers] what we needed most—his serious attention, his reasonable hopes, a real market" (x). Furthermore, says Munro, "He did all this for Canadian writing without ever putting on nationalistic blinkers" (x). In his memoir of the mentorship of Bernard Malamud, Clark Blaise writes that a true mentor has "the qualities of faith and patience" (37). He adds that: "The mentors that last in our lives are those who do not press a case, do not try to shape, or inflate; do not lust for miniatures of themselves, or even try to leave much of an impression at all" (40). This type of mentoring rings true of Robert Weaver, and the letters that are collected in the Munro archive—twelve of them, dated 1958 to 1979—tell a story in themselves, a story of a mentorship that went far beyond an occasional letter informing Munro that a story had been accepted or rejected. Weaver acts as editor, friend, motivator, adviser, referee, agent, father-figure, and conscience, to name a few of the roles detectable in the correspondence. As such a pervasive figure, he brings with him certain cultural advantages for the artist, as well as certain ideological pressures.

Weaver pushes Munro to apply for grants, for which he suggests and approaches referees, and agrees to act as one himself.
He accepts her work for broadcast on *Anthology* and also for
publication in the *Tamarack Review*. He also solicits Munro's
work for these two markets. He advises her on how to play the
game with American publishers, and it is Weaver who personally
approaches Jack McClelland in 1961 with five of her stories. It is
also Weaver who thereafter sends her work to Ryerson Press,
though seven years pass before Ryerson publishes *Dance of the
Happy Shades*. Once that publication is achieved, Weaver serves
as head of the English-language jury that selects *Dance of the
Happy Shades* as recipient of the 1968 Governor General's
Award. His support continues as Munro's career progresses, but
the tone of the letters changes perceptibly as Munro's reputation
and marketability rise. The correspondence eventually trails off
as publisher Douglas Gibson and Virginia Barber, Munro's
American literary agent, take over the mentoring role.

Bourdieu argues that "The art business, a trade in things that
have no price, belongs to the class of practices in which the logic
of the pre-capitalist economy lives on" (*Field* 75). The field of
cultural production is "the economic world reversed" (164), a
world that functions "only by virtue of a constant, collective
repression of narrowly 'economic' interest and of the real nature
of the practices revealed by 'economic' analysis" (74). One example of such "repression" is that, in Munro's archive, all files pertaining to finances are restricted to researchers and may be
viewed only by permission of the author. Another is the truism
that no accusation could be more damning to a serious artist, a
"literary" writer, than the accusation of commercialism. The
irony is that, ultimately, the "disinterestedness" of the serious
artist facilitates economic gain, because "Symbolic capital is to
be understood as economic or political capital that is disavowed,
misrecognized and thereby recognized, hence legitimate, a
'credit' which, under certain conditions, and always in the long
run, guarantees economic profits" (Bourdieu, *Field* 75). In short,
by disavowing the economic, by denying an interest in anything
but art for its own sake, the artist may make economic success

possible. (This is not to say that disavowal of the economic *ensures* economic success, however—Ethel Wilson, Ralph Connor, and Ernest Buckler come to mind—but rather that this disinterestedness is one of several "conditions" that must be in place for artistic consecration to occur.)

In the 1950s and 1960s, self-deprecating stories of the small size of the Canadian cultural audience abounded. For example, Sandy Stewart quotes Weaver as saying of *Anthology* that he was "the only producer who knew all of the show's listeners by their first names" (155).[3] Stewart then adds, however, that "In fact, the show had an audience that exceeded 52,000." Even more interestingly, Munro repeats an identical myth about the *Tamarack Review* in her 1992 interview with Jeanne McCulloch and Mona Simpson for the *Paris Review*: "It was a nice little magazine, a very brave magazine. The editor said he was the only editor in Canada who knew all his readers by their first names" (235). It is probable that such self-effacing mythology is partly what allows the "logic of the pre-capitalist economy" to function unproblematically in Weaver's mentorship of Canadian writers.

The cultural nationalism of the fifties led to the publishing phenomenon of the sixties, which was Munro's point of entry into Canadian literary culture. The place of the mentor in that particular cultural and historical moment is also crucial for, as Bourdieu argues, any study of cultural production must consider "not only the direct producers of the work in its materiality (artist, writer, etc.) but also the producers of the meaning and value of the work—critics, publishers, gallery directors and the whole set of agents whose combined efforts produce consumers capable of knowing and recognizing the work of art as such" (*Field* 37).

Central to this discussion is the question of artistic reputation and how it is built, a discussion tempered by a skepticism of myths of authorship as uncomplicated by external forces such as market economics and patronage. The theory of the author function defines the writer both as a subjected and resistant individual—that is, the author as agent is constantly shaped by, but also takes advantage of, and resists, the ideologies that affect her. One example of this process is Munro's desire to iden-

tify herself as a regional writer and to efface markers of
Canadian identity while at the same time functioning and publishing as a Canadian author. While the "Canadian" cultural factor is key in this chapter, it is important, also, to recognize the
interdependence of ideological pressures related to nationality,
gender, and genre, and bear that interdependence in mind as the
study draws out one ideological thread at a time. Finally, the discussion must maintain an awareness of the practical differences
between the established, entrenched culture of France, as
described by Bourdieu, with its centuries of history, nationalism,
and canon against the post-colonial self-consciousness of a
Canadian literature in the process of establishing its own legitimacy. One small example illustrates the difference: In October
1997, the Canadian writing community, aware that the venerable
Prairie author W.O. Mitchell was terminally ill, arranged a tribute
in Calgary, in conjunction with an annual writers' festival called
Wordfest. The tribute featured a dozen writers and commentators and was well attended by hundreds of Mitchell's fans. When
Mitchell died in March 1998, his passing prompted lengthy tributes in the major newspapers, brief obituaries on the national
television networks, and several discussions, tributes, and recol-
lections on CBC Radio. Mitchell's funeral was a private family
service, held in the small town of High River, Alberta, where he
had lived for many years. In France, in 1882, the eightieth birth-
day of Victor Hugo was celebrated by a parade of half a million
people who filed reverently past the author's window, as 5000
musicians played the French national anthem, *La Marseillaise.*
Upon Hugo's death three years later, public mourning was so
widespread and extravagant that "The crush of the funeral
crowds pushed a woman off a bridge to drown, together with the
man who tried to save her. Someone else gave birth" (Coles D10).
In her preface to *The Affair of Gabrielle Russier,* Mavis Gallant
describes French culture as one in which "literature is taught as
a way of life, almost as a substitute for experience...a society
where books are revered" (6). In Canada, a large percentage of
the population appears unaware that such a thing as Canadian
literature exists.[4]

In "Writers and Publishers in English-Canadian Literature," Frank Davey analyzes the Canadian literary marketplace with reference to Norman Feltes's work on the production of the Victorian novel, and remarks that literary publications in Canada in the nineteenth and the early twentieth century were what Feltes describes as " 'petty commodity productions' rather than capitalist productions" (94). In fact, according to Davey, despite the burgeoning of cultural nationalism and CanLit in the years after the Second World War,

> the petty-commodity mode remains the dominant form of literary publication in English Canada. Texts are written, even by experienced authors, with little conscious thought for the marketplace and with little input by publishers, whose staff generally lacks the man-power or talent to give such input. The audience inscribed in such texts, however, is a small, middle-class educated one, and very often with a regional or specifically ideological character. (95)

In the petty-commodity mode of production, therefore, the writer has the "autonomy" of a legitimate cultural producer. The "logic of the pre-capitalist economy" is tenable in such a market; obviously, the economic is easily disavowed when the stakes are extremely small. The small scale of the Canadian literary scene that Munro entered in the fifties is thus an important aspect of her self-formation as author.

However, Canada was not Munro's first choice for marketing her work. While studying at the University of Western Ontario in the early fifties, Munro published several of her stories in the student paper, *Folio*. These early successes prompted her to seek a wider audience—in the United States. In the *Paris Review* interview, Munro admits: "I sent all my early stories to *The New Yorker* in the 1950's, and then I stopped sending for a long time and sent only to magazines in Canada" (233). The fact that the author sent to Canadian markets by default is clear in her next remark: "*The New Yorker* sent me nice notes though—pencilled, informal messages. They never signed them. They weren't terribly encouraging. I still remember one of them: 'The writing is very nice, but the theme is a bit overly familiar'" (233).

Historically, the fifties and early sixties were "the dark ages of Canadian literature" (Crean 25) and especially "a dark period for writers of Canadian fiction" (Drainie 289). Furthermore, the cultural nationalism of the period was distinctly Tory in timbre, nostalgic for the certainties of empire, and suspicious of modernity in general and American consumerism and mass culture in particular (Buffie 234). Probably the most significant development during Munro's first decade of authorship was the Massey Commission's hearings on the arts, 1949-51, which came to the conclusion that the Canadian writer is "not sufficiently recognized" and suffers from "isolation." The commission saw itself as "entrusted with nothing less than the spiritual foundations of our national life" (qtd. in Pacey, "Writer" 18-19). In his analysis of Canadian culture in 1952, one year after the report of the Massey Commission, George Grant describes Canada as "about to be swept into the maelstrom of American imperialism" (qtd. in Bissell 8). In response to the Massey hearings, government support and subsidization of the arts were entrenched. The National Library of Canada was founded in 1953. The major journals, the *Canadian Forum, Fiddlehead,* and several university quarterlies, continued, while the *Tamarack Review* (1956), under the editorship of Robert Weaver, and *Prism* (1959) were added to the cultural scene. The academic study of the national literature got a boost in 1959 with the founding of *Canadian Literature* at the University of British Columbia.

For better or worse, the culture-building trends of the fifties did provide an opening, however limited and parochial, for a writer like Alice Munro. Though her Canada Council grant applications were unsuccessful until she was well established in her career,[5] journals like *Tamarack Review* and *Canadian Forum* provided noncommercial markets for her work, as did the Canadian Broadcasting Corporation radio program *Anthology*. In Canada, at this point in its history, the lack of a commercial market was at least partly compensated for by the cultural engines of the government and the academy.

In "The Writer and His Public (1920-1960)," Desmond Pacey notes that in the postwar years,

> Canada still had no writer of the first rank by world standards, was still unsure whether her writers should seek to be cosmopolitan or to develop an indigenous tradition, was still prone either to under-rate Canadian books because they were not reviewed in the fashionable English or American periodicals or to over-rate them because they were our own, still alternated between truculent cultural self-assertion and whining cultural self-pity. ("Writer" 21)

In his review of Canadian fiction from 1940 to 1960, Hugo McPherson concurs, saying that despite the bleatings of "Canada-in-excelsis patriots" (205), Canadian literature had still not come of age; he comments on how Canadian fiction has profited from writers who have gone abroad, citing Laurence, Gallant, and Richler. He praises the latter's "brash rejection of Canada's imported and inherited pieties" (225).

Though Munro was not a nationalist by temperament, neither was she an expatriate in either residence or subject matter. In other words, despite her reluctance to embrace "CanLit," she remained fundamentally Canadian in her life and in her work. While other writers acquired cosmopolitan dash abroad, Munro was at home in West Coast suburbs, raising children and doing laundry. And in her fiction, Munro almost never left the country, or the contemporary period, for that matter, until her writing career was well established.

By the seventies, the rising tide of Canadian literary voices makes defining true Canadian-ness a concern. In the introduction to his 1973 survey of Canadian writers, *From There to Here*, Frank Davey addresses the problem of Canadian-ness by choosing to include only writers who are Canadian either by "birth or residence" (10). He also excludes those who are recent immigrants writing primarily of their homeland, such as Jane Rule or Robin Skelton, and he furthermore excludes "expatriates who choose to enter fully into the literary traditions of other cultures," such as Mavis Gallant (10). By Davey's criteria, Laurence and Richler can be counted as Canadian because, unlike Gallant, they write about Canadian communities, even though they reside in England.

Margaret Atwood appears to take a similar position. In a scathing review of the first Canadian short story collection published in the United States, Alec Lucas's *Great Canadian Short Stories*, Atwood accuses the editor of believing that "'internationalism' is synonymous with good writing and 'Canadian' with provincialism" (63). She objects to the inclusion of authors such as Malcolm Lowry and Brian Moore, particularly because the stories selected were neither set in nor written in Canada; for Atwood, "It's annoying to find Canada being given credit for literary talents it had nothing to do with forming" (63). She further objects to the selection of a Clark Blaise story about the American South, rather than an "eminently more suitable" (64) selection about Blaise's mixed Prairie Protestant and Quebec Catholic parents. Obviously, Atwood's criteria for Canadian-ness include residence or birth *plus* subject matter.

The need for cultural self-definition in this period creates a see-saw conflict between nationalism and internationalism, flag-waving versus sophistication. James Polk's review of *Lives of Girls and Women* illustrates the dilemma. Polk comments that the text follows "the universal pattern for a first novel, although the British might require more misery at public school, the French more adultery, the Americans more violence" (102). In short, the novel is universal in design and subject, but Canadian in its muted approach to elitism, immorality, and brutality. But for Polk, the novel's success arises from its very regionality, its view of "Ontario social myths from the bottom up" (102). He sees Munro's Jubilee as a hybrid of "Faulkner's Jefferson and Wuthering Heights" (103)—in short, this Canadian novel's regionalism achieves the universal. However, Polk then closes his review with the following bit of boosterism: "If the novel falls short of its own ambitions, it is a remarkable book nonetheless and should be purchased (not borrowed from the library but paid for) by those who want something good to read for a change, and by those who are interested in the development of one of Canada's foremost prose writers" (104). The nationalistic subtext is evident: support your local author both despite and because of her Canadian-ness.

In a similar vein, two reviews of the third series of Robert Weaver's Oxford anthology of Canadian stories (in which a Munro story appears, as in all five series) show evidence of the nationalist/universalist dilemma. Len Gasparini praises the "universality of human emotions manifest in the best writers" in this collection (C5), while the Ken Adachi review bears the headline "Turn Off the TV and Read a Story!" (D7). Such an exhortation appearing in a review of, say, *Best American Short Stories* or a new Norton edition would be out of place and unnecessary, but for incipient CanLit a certain amount of boosterism appears to be in order.

That cultural nationalism in literature remained an issue even in the nineties is evident from an article by Russell Smith in the *Globe and Mail* book review section in 1994. Smith describes how he turned down an offer to review a Canadian first novel, because "I didn't want to say publicly why I thought it was bad" (C5). He confesses to being torn between national pride and high literary standards: " I sympathize with book review editors. How to deal with the ever-swelling tide of Canadian literary books? You do too many and you're not catering to your general-interest readership, which doesn't actually read too many of them.[6] You do too few and you get excoriated by the Canon crows for Philistinism and not nurturing home-grown art and culture" (C5). However, Smith also insists that he wants "to judge the Canadian literary novel in the context of global literature since Homer, not in the context of other Canadian novels" (C5). Thus he makes the unhappy compromise of simply refusing to write a bad review of a fellow Canadian novelist and is "suckered into writing this essay instead" (C5). Munro herself appears to be aware of the enclosed world of CanLit, for though she refuses to espouse cultural nationalism, she is still affected by its power, and by the closed circle of the Canadian cultural market. In her 1996 interview with Peter Gzowski, promoting *Selected Stories,* she declines to name which Canadian authors she prefers, for fear of omitting the name of someone whose work she admires.[7] She then goes on to mention a selection of Irish and American writers she reads and enjoys, apparently not fearful of offending writers outside Canada's borders. Even when attempting to avoid the subject, Munro is nonetheless influenced by the requirements of cultural nationalism.

Back in the seventies, Munro was considered one of the three major women writers in Canada, sharing the spotlight with Margaret Laurence and Margaret Atwood. Of the three, Munro is singular in her disavowal of nationalist interests and political activism. Two articles in a 1987 issue of *Books in Canada* illustrate her singularity. The first is a tribute to the late Margaret Laurence, which abounds with nationalistic subtext. For example, the article quotes descriptions of Laurence as "the heart and guts of the writing community in this country" and "'creative godmother' to such writers as Margaret Atwood, Marian Engel, and Audrey Thomas" as well as "a creative forebear of Alice Munro" ("Margaret Laurence" 3). According to the *Books in Canada* tribute, Laurence was "A central figure in the wave of cultural nationalism that surrounded Canada's centennial and the publishing boom of the 1970's," and "With her death, Canada's writers have lost the matriarch of what she liked to describe as 'the tribe'" (3). Laurence's deep commitment to the cause of Canadian literature is well known, and is evident in a convocation address made ten years before her death:

> The calibre and scope of our literature now is such that it can be read and taught simply because it is interesting, worth reading and worth teaching. But for us it has an added dimension as well. It is our own; it speaks to us, through its many and varied voices, of things which are close to our hearts; it links us with our ancestors and with one another....[We do] have a great need to possess our own land, to know our own heritage, to value ourselves in relation to a world community. (qtd. in C. Thomas 103)

Interestingly, the same *Books in Canada* issue that contains the Laurence tribute also includes a piece called "Writers' Writers," which surveys a group of Canadian authors on two questions: What are you reading this winter, and what are your thoughts on the current state of Canadian literature? Mentioned in the Laurence tribute is the belief that, in early 1987,

"Canadian writing now finds itself at a bit of a plateau in its development" (3), which serves to explain the impetus for the second question. In any event, Munro's *The Progress of Love* is on reading lists for writers including Margaret Atwood, Sandra Birdsell, Timothy Findley, Jack Hodgins, Irving Layton, John Metcalf, and Audrey Thomas, while Munro's literary selection is *The Elizabeth Stories* by Isabel Huggan. The surveyed authors also make a variety of comments on Canadian literature. Atwood's is as follows:

> Are the government's recent intentions merely stupidity or some sort of scorched-earth policy? That is, wipe out Canadian culture first, and then there won't be anyone left to protest when sell-Canada-down-the-river free trade deals are announced. Don't they realize that if everything becomes homogeneous we will cease to see the necessity of paying for a government that has rendered itself superfluous? ("Writers' Writers" 8)

Munro's comments on the state of "CanLit" are somewhat different; she says, "I never think about things like that, and consider it a waste of time for a writer to do so" (10).

Munro's discomfort with discussions of and pronouncements on Canadian literature is evident in her 1994 *Morningside* interview with Peter Gzowski. The host confesses that he'd been told Munro was a difficult subject, but that after their first interview, he found her very accommodating. Munro laughs and says, "That's because you didn't ask me about CanLit!" Even in this brief exchange, it is evident that Munro dislikes the role of spokesperson for national culture. Part of this dislike undoubtedly stems from the disavowal of the economic and political that is a part of her self-construction as author. For Munro, the label of "regional writer" is more comfortable than the politically active label of Canadian cultural worker, possibly because the "disinterestedness" of the former fits her own definition of literary seriousness; according to Bourdieu, refusal of the political is certainly an identifying feature for producers in the field of restricted production, of "serious" art.[8] Though Munro is reluctant to espouse nationalism, she willingly describes herself as a

regionalist: "If I'm a regional writer, the region I'm writing about
has many things in common with the American South....A closed
rural society with a pretty homogeneous Scotch-Irish racial
strain going slowly to decay" (Struthers, "South" 29).

Why does Munro take a different position on cultural nationalism than her contemporary peers? Part of the reason may be
the insecurity engendered by her long apprenticeship. Robert
Weaver has commented that "there have been times during her
career when a writer with less determination and fewer natural
gifts might have been frustrated to the point of being silenced
altogether" (*Oxford* 1973 325). I would also argue that Munro's
regionalism is partly linked to issues of class. Bourdieu points
out that "a faulty sense of investment, linked to social distance
(among writers from the working class or the *petite bourgeoisie*)
or geographical distance (among provincials and foreigners)
inclines beginners to aim for the dominant positions" (*Field* 68).
Though class structures in the New World are not as rigid and
institutionalized as those in Western Europe, Munro's awareness of class and her own definition of her class position play
an important role in her authorship. Munro's earliest stories,
such as "The Dimensions of a Shadow" or "A Basket of
Strawberries," show the strong influence of Joyce's very dominant *Dubliners.* However, when socially or geographically marginalized beginners confront the snobberies of the cultural
field, they are often impelled to "accept themselves for what
they are and, like Courbet, to mark themselves positively with
what is stigmatized—their provincial accent, dialect, 'proletar-
ian' style, etc.—but the more strongly, the less successful their
initial attempts at *assimilation* have been" (Bourdieu, *Field* 70).
I suspect that a large part of Munro's regionalism arises from
her long and often frustrating apprenticeship, complete with
refused Canada Council applications and *The New Yorker* rejections of stories with "overly familiar" themes, as well as subtle
class bias and obvious genre bias. Genre is less of an issue with
both Atwood and Laurence, as they work primarily in the
"higher" genres—the novel in both cases, and poetry in
Atwood's. Class is less of an issue as well, if one considers edu-

cation as one of the markers of social position, as Bourdieu certainly does, seeing education as one type of "symbolic violence of the dominant over the dominated," along with "workplace relationships, social organisations, even...conceptions of good taste and beauty" (Harker, Mahar, and Wilkes 5). Munro completed two years of study in English literature at the University of Western Ontario from 1949 to 1951—admittedly a significant level of higher education for a woman of her generation. However, "after her two year scholarship ran out, she couldn't afford a third year at university" (C. Ross 49); she married Jim Munro in December 1951.

Munro's father, Robert Laidlaw, dropped out of Blyth Continuation School "to pursue the solitary life of hunting and trapping in the bush" (C. Ross 29). Laidlaw was "a failed fox farmer, a failed turkey farmer, and a security guard, amongst other things" ("Writing's Something I Did" E1). Munro's mother, Anne Chamney, fought for an independent life as a school-teacher, and had social and intellectual ambitions, but the combination of marriage and motherhood, the Depression, and Parkinson's disease defeated her aspirations. Munro grew up on the outskirts of Wingham, in a "rural slum" (C. Ross 23) called Lower Town, described by Munro as "outside the whole social structure...this kind of little ghetto where all the bootleggers and prostitutes and hangers-on lived....It was a community of outcasts. I had that feeling about myself" (qtd. in C. Ross 23).

Whatever an individual's biographical data suggests about class, what is crucially important is the subject's (internal, perceived) self-construction of class position and the social construction of same (particularly slippery in the supposedly "class-less" New World, in which Jack is as good as his master); furthermore, these two (self- and social) constructions are often at odds with each other. Certainly, Munro sees herself as "out of any mainstream" and "from a lower class" (McCulloch and Simpson 257). Munro's regionalism could well be linked to her own sense of marginalization arising from an (imagined or actual) inferior class position; in other words, in the "plurality of selves" that define the author function, one important "self" in

Munro's self-construction as author is that of a person lacking certain socioeconomic advantages.

The position-taking of "regionalist," however, risks further marginalization. In *Keywords,* Raymond Williams points out that the label of "regionalist"

> can, like dialect, be used to indicate a "subordinate" or "infe-
> rior" form, as in *regional accent*, which implies that there is
> somewhere (and not only in a class) a "national accent." But
> in a *regional novel* there can be simple acknowledgement of
> a distinct place and way of life, though probably more often
> this is also a limiting judgement. It is interesting that a novel
> set in the Lake District or in Cornwall is very often called
> regional, whereas one set in London or New York is not. This
> overlaps with the important *metropolitan-provincial* cultural
> distinction…provincial and regional are terms of relative infe-
> riority to an assumed centre, in dominant usage. (265)

If Williams is correct, then why does Munro appear to prefer the label of "regionalist" over "Canadian"? It is possible that in placing her work alongside that of the great regionalists of the American South, such as Faulkner, McCullers, Welty, and O'Connor, Munro believes that she will transcend her own Canadian-ness, and achieve "universal" authorial status. As Beverly Rasporich notes, regionalists, by working out of the detail of the local, "can communicate the particular *as* universal…they and their readers [can] be imaginatively transported into a powerfully engaging and seemingly all encompassing fictive space" (122). Besides, it is one of the ironies of artistic life in a small cultural milieu like Canada that "Canadian" is itself all too often equated with "inferior" or "provincial," and that a Canadian artist, whether a musician, actor, or writer, does not truly achieve what Foucault calls the author function until s/he is accorded international, particularly American, acclaim. In Bronwyn Drainie's 1988 biography of her actor father, *Living the Part: John Drainie and the Dilemma of Canadian Stardom*, the author remarks how in Canada, the "meritocracy" of the acting profession is skewed by the power of the CBC. According to Drainie, "in Canada, until very recently, [the] basic laws of the marketplace did not apply" (12). What she says of the acting profession is, I think, equally true of the writing profession.

In any case, despite her disavowal of "CanLit," Munro benefited greatly from the cultural nationalism of the fifties and sixties, a movement that opened doors for many new writers. The cultural milieu that Munro attempted to enter in the 1950s and 1960s was small, underfunded, enclosed. Though Munro had some success in selling her stories to mass-market publications like *Chatelaine*, it took the influence of a powerful mentor, Robert Weaver, to establish her literary reputation in Canada.

The earliest available letter from Weaver in the Munro archive at the University of Calgary is dated 12 December 1958, addressed to Mrs Alice Munro in West Vancouver. The letter begins: "I've spoken to one or two people here who have had something to do with fellowship applications, and we all seem to feel that you might as well apply to the Canada Council without worrying about what Daniells and his people may decide" (MsC 37.2.8.3). Weaver is advising Munro to apply for a Canada Council writer's grant, despite the fact that she apparently has another application in elsewhere, probably for a provincial arts grant juried by Roy Daniells of the University of British Columbia. The tone of the letter mixes power and knowledge with humility and hesitation; Weaver knows people who know about these things, but he softens his statements with phrases like "we all seem to feel" and "you might as well." He goes on to justify applying to two granting agencies: "For one thing I think that they're very slow and may take a long time. I know also that he [Daniells] had a fairly extensive group of writers on his list. If you should by any wild good luck be offered both awards we could figure out at that time how to get you out of the embarrassment" (MsC 37.2.8.3). In any case, Weaver's message is that lots of other writers are vying for the same money, so she should not put all her eggs in one basket. In the next paragraph, Weaver takes a more active role:

> I will telephone Murdo Mackinnon tonight or over the weekend and see whether he will write a letter for you and tell him

where to send it. I'll also write a letter myself this weekend.
I'll speak to Milton Wilson at the *Canadian Forum* and see
whether he remembers your stories well enough to write
something for you. I'm not sure about the situation at
*Chatelaine* since Gladys Shinner has now left the magazine,
but I know Doris McGibbon, the editor, quite well and I'll see
whether she is in a position to do anything for you. (MsC
37.2.8.3)

The courtly hesitancy of the first paragraph is undercut by the
down-to-business tone of the second, showing Weaver as a mentor who can summon powerful allies. The reference to Milton
Wilson's not remembering Munro's stories is puzzling, as the
*Canadian Forum* published a Munro story each year from 1954
through 1957. *Chatelaine* published Munro several times during
the fifties; her stories appeared in March 1956, July 1956, and
July 1957.

Having thus covered the Ontario scene, Weaver continues:
"There may be people in Vancouver who would be worth
approaching and that, of course, I'll leave up to you" (MsC
37.2.8.3). It is noteworthy that in the entire letter, this is the
only point where Weaver is willing to leave matters in Munro's
hands. In a biography for one of his many anthologies, he mentions that Munro "applied for grants but was unsuccessful
because people with literary influence even in Vancouver were
unaware of her work" (*Oxford* 1973, 325). Interestingly, Munro
demurs on this point. She says that the reason she did not get
grants was that she asked for money for babysitters and cleaning ladies, rather than for a research trip to some exotic locale,
as male writers did (C. Ross 58).

The letter concludes: "I'm glad you don't mind my interfering
but I did begin to think that the time was fairly short and we
might as well work every angle we can in whatever time does
remain" (MsC 37.2.8.3). The language of these closing lines is an
intriguing mixture of apology and scolding. The message
appears to be that he had to "interfere" because Munro had not
done what was necessary to meet the deadlines and somebody
had to make sure that this application was prepared on time.

Weaver is a master of understatement in this letter. He expresses his support and concern in fatherly tones, yet the power he exerts in initiating award applications, naming referees, and generally taking charge of this business is considerable. In a small, inbred cultural community like Canada in the 1950s, the support of a powerful, knowledgeable mentor, one who has experience and connections, is crucial to the artist's survival. The economic and cultural limitations of the Canadian literary marketplace tend to make Robert Weaver's position less apparently equivocal than that of most "symbolic bankers."

The next letter is dated 24 August 1961, slightly less than three years later. There has been a bit of a publication drought for Munro since "Sunday Afternoon" appeared in the *Canadian Forum* in September 1957, though in real-life terms, this period marks the birth of Munro's second child and the death of her mother. In any event, the next publication comes in the spring of 1960 when "The Peace of Utrecht" appears in Weaver's *Tamarack Review*. Weaver also edited *Ten for Wednesday Night*, in which "The Trip to the Coast" (retitled "A Trip to the Coast" in *Dance of the Happy* Shades) appeared in 1961. Early in 1961, Munro had discovered another market for her work in the *Montrealer*, which published her stories in February 1961, May 1961, September 1962, December 1964, and May 1965. Whether Weaver played any part in finding this market for Munro is unknown. Weaver's second letter begins again on a personal note, referring to "another visit" and commiserating that Jim and Alice's "bookstore deal seems to be stalled" (MsC 37.2.8.4), a reference to the couple's plan to purchase a bookselling business in Victoria.

The business part of the letter begins in the second paragraph, in which Weaver apologizes for the delay in sending a packet of stories to Jack McClelland. Weaver explains that both he and McClelland have been travelling on business and have had trouble connecting, thus drawing attention to the busy schedules of both, and the connections of Weaver himself. The letter goes on to say that McClelland "is at least interested in the idea of publishing perhaps half a dozen of the stories and I think

he should be given some chance now to make a firm decision"
(MsC 37.2.8.4). Weaver makes it clear that Jack McClelland
should be given top priority, despite the likelihood of rejection,
suggested by "at least" and "perhaps." He afterwards softens the
impending blow (McClelland's rejection letter is dated October
1961) by saying that should McClelland and Stewart turn the stories down, Weaver himself may attempt to publish them through
*Tamarack*; failing that, he says, he has already put out a few
feelers with an English publisher. As Buffie points out, the cultural nationalism of the period is characterized by a Tory attach-
ment to the Old Country, matched with a certain distaste for,
and suspicion of, American mass culture. It's likely that
Weaver's eagerness to place Munro's work with either a
Canadian or an English publisher reflects that ideology.

Indeed, Weaver's protectionism is apparent in the next paragraph: "Where does this leave you with Mr. Watmough and his
firm in the United States? This sounds to me a little like a fish-
ing expedition on his part since they would have a very tough
time *introducing a completely unknown short story writer to an
American audience*" [emphasis added]. Though Weaver has
acknowledged the importance of the American market as early
as 1956,[9] the difficulty of cracking the American market is clear;
Munro did not manage to publish in the United States until the
mid-1970s.[10] What is striking, though, is the almost uncanny
resemblance between Weaver's warning and the language of the
actual rejection letter it anticipates: the rejection letter from
Theodore Purdy at Appleton Century Crofts mentions "the difficulty of selling volumes of collected short stories unless the
author's name is already well known" (MsC 37.2.1). Obviously,
genre biases in the book trade are well entrenched on both sides
of the border.

The next part of Weaver's letter offers this lesson in literary
marketing:

> I think that perhaps you should write to Watmough and tell
> him that six of the stories have actually been submitted to
> McClelland and Stewart who have shown at least some
> interest. You might offer to get in touch with him as soon as

> you have heard from Jack or me, or you might offer to send
> him a few of your stories just as long as he keeps in mind
> that there is a formal investigation going on somewhere else.
> If he really wants the book, who knows but that he might then
> get in touch with M&S and of course that would do you no
> harm. In any case try to be a little evasive right now and keep
> him on the string. (MsC 37.2.8.4)

Weaver repeats the phrase "at least" in discussing McClelland's interest here, and uses mediating words like "I think," "perhaps," and "you might"; his language is never imperative, never falsely flattering or pushy. But the survival skills he offers here are crucial: 1) Canada first: your best chances of publication, for now, are here; 2) if a publisher thinks that somebody else wants your work he's more likely to want it for himself; 3) the multiple submission game is slightly different for awards than it is for publishers, but the principle of never putting all your eggs in one basket still holds. It's also important to note that in the proposed McClelland and Stewart deal, Weaver puts himself in a position to help two friends at once. The irony is that, in the late seventies and early eighties, McClelland and Stewart attempted to sign Munro (MsC 38.2.63.61). It was only when her Macmillan editor, Doug Gibson, moved there that she agreed to follow.

Weaver's letter closes with the following promise: "I'll see about an agent in October when I'm in New York and I'll be in touch with you soon" (37.2.8.4). Munro is at the point in her career when she wants to find an agent and seriously wants U.S. publication; however, more than a decade passes before she does either of these things. Indeed, Weaver's letters contain no further reference to the task of finding a literary agent for Munro, though subsequent correspondence makes it clear that he is functioning in precisely that capacity himself. It should be noted that in a small cultural milieu, one figure takes on many, sometimes conflicting, roles.

Certainly, the next four letters in the archive show Weaver functioning as literary agent. In a letter dated 29 August 1961, five days after the previous one, Weaver sends Munro a sheaf of copies of reviews of his 1960 anthology for Oxford; a month later, a CBC–TV producer, prompted by Weaver, invites Munro to submit a teleplay (MsC 37.2.8.6); and in a letter dated 8 November 1961, Weaver asks: "I wonder if you have seen the new monthly, 'Exchange,' being published in Montreal. I am enclosing a copy of it and you might keep it in mind as another market for stories, since it is paying about $100 for fiction as long as it lasts" (MsC 37.2.8.7). The first letter reminds Munro of his support of her work; the second offers another market within the CBC; the third releases Munro to the larger world of the open literary market, but Weaver warns that, as a potential market, *Exchange* will probably be short-lived. Val Ross, in a profile of Weaver, indicates just how lucrative a market the CBC was for a writer in the sixties: "What Weaver paid writers for contributing to one program was often more than the advances publishers paid for their books" (A9). Weaver thus encourages Munro to try her wings, yet warns her of the poverty of the market at the same time, thus presenting her with a serious double bind. The letter closes with an offhand remark that really undercuts the *Exchange* information: "incidentally, I'd very much like to have a new story of yours for the Spring issue of *Tamarack* and I wonder if you are going to send something soon" (MsC 37.2.8.7). Apparently, though, Munro did not send to either *Exchange* or *Tamarack* that year. No publications in the former are listed, and Munro's next *Tamarack* publication was not until 1968.

An important aspect of Weaver's mentorship is that he maintained contact with Munro even when she was not producing work. In her Foreword to *The* Anthology *Anthology*, Munro mentions Weaver's business letters, but then she adds: "He also wrote me letters when I hadn't sent him anything, when I hadn't written anything, and it was these letters, especially, that gave me nourishment and hope. I had very barren times. Most young writers do" (ix). It is in this sense, more than any other, that Weaver's essentially conservative, cultural nationalist mentorship is different from that of publisher Douglas Gibson, agent Virginia Barber, or publisher's editor Ann Close. For Weaver truly has very little to gain, financially, from Munro's success or failure. His interest in her, his faith in her, is not about mass culture or profit and loss. That he would take the time to write an encouraging letter to a young housewife and mother too exhausted to pick up a pen is an indication of his function as a culture-builder and cultural nationalist. Bourdieu comments on how, according to the "charismatic ideology" of literary production, "the 'great' dealers, the 'great' publishers, are inspired talent-spotters who, guided by their disinterested, unreasoning passion for a work of art, have 'made' the painter or writer, or have helped him make himself, by encouraging him in difficult moments with the faith they had in him, guiding him with their advice and freeing him from material worries" (77). This "charismatic ideology" of the disinterested "talent-spotter" is part of Weaver's construction as Canadian cultural banker. Frank Davey points out how the petty-commodity mode dominates Canadian publishing; it is easy to see how, in this "pre-capitalist" economy, the illusions of "autonomy" and "disinterestedness" are relatively easily maintained.

Weaver writes to Munro again on 22 November 1961, two weeks after he requested a story for the *Tamarack Review*, to finalize arrangements to publish "The Peace of Utrecht" in an upcoming anthology that he will edit. The most interesting part of this letter is the following: "Ryerson Press want to see the five short stories since they are trying to find some work by younger writers and obviously intend generally to improve their publishing program. I am going to assume that you won't mind and send the five stories to a friend of mine at Ryerson Press" (MsC 37.2.8.8). The history of the "five stories" mentioned in this document opens up a view of how myths of authorial apprenticeship are constructed. In their introduction to the Munro selection in the classroom text *An Anthology of Canadian Literature in English*, Donna Bennett and Russell Brown repeat a familiar cultural myth about writers and their craft: they suggest that because Munro is a "slow and meticulous craftsman, she did not publish her first collection of stories...until 1968" (300). Certainly, Munro *is* slow and meticulous, rarely producing more than three or four stories per year, and a new collection every four years, the one exception being the pressure-cooker period following the publication of *Dance of the Happy Shades* (1968), in which she pushed herself to produce a novel, *Lives of Girls and Women* (1971), in three years, and then a second collection of stories just three years later, *Something I've Been Meaning to Tell You* (1974).[11] However, Bennett and Brown may be in error when they cite meticulous craft as the primary reason why Munro did not publish her first book until she was in her mid-thirties.

Part of what the archive does is to give the lie to the notion that authorial intention resides in the published version of a work. The archive is a space where the juncture of ideological pressures that underlie authorship are legible, for, as Pierre Bourdieu comments, "Specifically aesthetic conflicts about the legitimate vision of the world—in the last resort about what deserves to be represented and the right way to represent it— are political conflicts (appearing in their most euphemized form) for the power to impose the dominant definition of reality, and social reality in particular" (*Field* 101). In short, Munro's "legitimate vision of the world" comes in short story form; yet her right to represent the world in that form is in conflict with the economic imperatives of the cultural field. The archive shows that Munro attempted to get a collection of her short fiction published in book form as early as 1961. When Theodore Purdy rejects Munro's stories in a letter dated 26 September 1961, he praises her work, saying that "many of these stories were extremely well done and the variety of subjects covered was another encouraging factor"; but then, as noted, he mentions how tough it is to sell a short story collections by an unknown writer (MsC 37.2.1), and he asks whether she has written or is working on a novel. Less than three weeks later, Munro receives another rejection letter, this time from a Canadian publisher. Jack McClelland likewise refers to the "age-old book trade legend" about the difficulty of marketing short story collections, and asks "But what about the novel? How is it progressing? Can we be of any help?" (MsC 37.2.22.1).

While the issue of genre is explored in detail in chapter 4, I offer these letters now as a way of contextualizing Bennett and Brown's assertion that the reason for Munro's delayed first publication was primarily her craftsmanship. Her failure to publish actually included a complex system of domestic realities—Munro was the mother of young children, for one thing—in addition to sociohistorical conditions such as genre bias and a cultural market so limited in size that the editor of a literary journal is said to know all of his subscribers by name. The literary canon is an ideological formation, and in order to enter it, an author is subject to its ideological pressures. The ideological pressures in the foregoing two letters are obvious: novels are better (more marketable) than short stories, and a "variety of subjects" is better than a narrow focus. For a writer like Munro, with her intense focus on a single point of view and a single region, as well her generic strength in the short story form, these pressures are very intense.

The stories mentioned in Weaver's letter of 22 November are doubtless the same five recently rejected by Appleton and by McClelland and Stewart. Playing the role of agent, Weaver "assumes" that Munro "won't mind" his submitting her work to Ryerson. The cultural insider in the small milieu, Weaver knows the future goals of the company and has a "friend" on the staff. Though Weaver's October trip to New York, during which he was to seek an agent for Munro, has already taken place, he makes no mention of this search. Instead, in this letter, Weaver certainly acts like a literary agent, only without demanding a commission. However, as agent, he can only offer her the Canadian scene where he has expertise, knowledge, and some power.

The agent's role is also evident in Weaver's cautious prodding of Munro in the final paragraph of this letter, in which he acknowledges the growing necessity of cracking the American market but reveals his less-than-expert position in this regard: "Some time this winter if you get a story done which you feel is one of your better ones, why don't you make a concerted attempt to publish in one of the better U.S. magazines? If this idea interests you at all, I could give you a list of the magazines I'd suggest and you could change or add to it, and then simply keep the story going around to see what, if any, comment you would get on it" (MsC 37.2.8.8). Here Weaver's limitations as agent of Canadian culture are evident. In terms of assistance, all Munro can expect is a list (and not an authoritative one) of magazine titles—as opposed to the "friends" and insider connections he can muster on the Canadian scene. Furthermore, Weaver anticipates failure, suggesting that Munro will be lucky to get more than a form rejection letter.

The latter part of the paragraph touches on the subject of genre. At this point in her career, Munro is struggling to produce a novel, which is understandable, given such rejections as those from Appleton Century Crofts and McClelland and Stewart. In a gentle and fatherly tone, Weaver encourages Munro to continue in the short story, possibly because it is his area of expertise, possibly because in Canadian terms it is a respected and relatively marketable form, or possibly because, even at this early stage, he knows where Munro's strength lies—and indeed, he appears to have been right on the latter score. In any case, what he says is "I don't know what to say to you at the moment about the novel problem but if you don't feel anxious [about] or even capable of writing a good novel right now and do feel ready to keep on with the short stories, I'd spend the winter in shorter fiction" (MsC 37.2.8.8.). Catherine Sheldrick Ross, too, writing in *Alice Munro: A Double Life*, characterizes 1961 as an extremely difficult year for Munro, during which she "became increasingly depressed by rejection letters," got an ulcer, and engaged in "a fierce attempt to will a novel into being" (61). But the attempt backfired and the only work Munro produced during this year was "The Office," a story about a woman who rents office space in order to take herself seriously as a writer, but finds herself regarded with suspicion by her landlord, overwhelmed by her own guilt and insecurity, and so distracted by her new surroundings that she gives up her office, the irony being that all this failure produces the story called "The Office." According to biographer Ross, "This period of blocked energy, when she felt seized up and unable to write anything at all, was the low point of her life" (61).

In "Writers and Publishers in English-Canadian Literature," Frank Davey argues that "the material conditions of book production act as determinants of the kinds of texts authors create" (99). The material conditions of the eventual production of Munro's first book, *Dance of the Happy Shades*, are revealing in terms of the author function in general and Weaver's mentorship in particular. Although seven years pass between the letter in which Weaver offers to send five stories to Ryerson, and his next letter to appear in the archive, Weaver's involvement can be pieced together from other sources.

In November 1961, Weaver's plan to approach Ryerson resulted in a letter to Munro from John Robert Colombo, undated, but identified by the author herself as pre-1963.[12] It begins: "A year ago, Dr John Webster Grant, the Senior Editor, wrote you about publishing a collection of your stories. In fact, manuscript copies of some of the stories are still in Ryerson's vault" (MsC 37.2.39.1). The letter from Dr Grant is not collected in the archive, but one can assume that Grant's letter was dated late 1961, since it was in the fall of that year that Weaver offered to send Munro's stories to a friend at Ryerson. Having mentioned that Munro's work has been sitting in the vault for at least a year, Colombo then goes on to say, "We are eager to publish your stories" (37.2.39.1). However, his eagerness is somewhat belied by the fact that the next letter from Ryerson is dated 1967, about five years later. What went on in those intervening years? Did Munro simply not respond? That seems unlikely, given her obvious desire to have a collection published. Had she stopped writing, had she lost confidence, had she been abandoned by Weaver? Did Ryerson know it could take its time, there being no competitor in the small Canadian market? Or did Ryerson lose interest, or run out of money? Was it Weaver who got the project on the rails again? The only one of these questions for which the archive provides an answer is the last one.

Catherine Sheldrick Ross describes the breakthrough that resulted in Munro's first book publication as follows: "Alice Munro was scarcely known outside literary circles when Earle Toppings of Ryerson Press wrote in 1967, inviting her to put together a collection of stories for a book" (64). The outlines of this story reflect what Catherine Belsey calls the bias of traditional literary history, in which "the process of production is called creation, a mystical and mysterious occurrence conceived rather as a state of mind than as work" (126-27). In this myth, literary genius does not calculate, negotiate, or ingratiate; an author creates, tells the truth about experience, and the receptive public recognizes her genius. The reader does not hear about the hard work, the endless drafts and rejections, the desperate periods of block, the effort to integrate one's own vision with the real demands of the marketplace. As Bourdieu writes, "attention to the *apparent producer*, the painter, writer, or composer, in short, the 'author,' suppress[es] the question of what authorizes the author, what creates the authority with which authors authorize" (76). When attention is focused on the genius of the author, the ideologies that underlie authorship are concealed. Thus, in Ross's account we receive the myth of the "discovery" of talent.

The archive contains only one 1967 letter from Earle Toppings, and it is obviously not an unbidden "invitation." Toppings is responding to the receipt of two new stories, namely "Postcard" and "Walker Brothers Cowboy," and says he is "very pleased" (MsC 37.2.39.1). He also remarks that he will be sending copies of the two new stories to Bob Weaver, clearly indicating that Munro's mentor is very much involved in this "invitation" to publish. Weaver's continued involvement with this first book extends to the Governor General's Award it ultimately received. The archive contains a press release forwarded to Munro by her publisher, which names the panel of jurors for the award as including Alberta novelist and academic Henry Kreisel and critic Philip Stratford of Montreal; but the head of the English language jury for that year is none other than Robert Weaver himself (MsC 37.2.39.4).

In Weaver's letter of 5 November 1968, in which he encloses a photocopy of a review of *Dance of the Happy Shades*, he also solicits more material from Munro for the expanded one-hour version of the radio program *Anthology*, and he encourages her to keep writing. Interestingly, he remarks "Now that you have begun to write some new stories once more, I hope you will keep at it" (MsC 37.2.8.9). Of all the figures from the literary marketplace, Weaver stands alone in his stalwart support of Munro's chosen genre. The next work published by the author is the 1971 novel *Lives of Girls and Women*. One can only surmise that Munro was at this point refusing to call her new work a novel—in fact, to this day, she describes it as an "episodic novel" (Struthers, "Real" 14)—given the enormous difficulties and near-breakdown caused by her efforts to produce a novel earlier in the decade.

Another long gap ensues in the Munro/Weaver correspondence, following the publication of *Dance of the Happy Shades*. In March 1973, Weaver writes to enclose a story manuscript that had been broadcast on *Anthology* ("Forgiveness in Families," 10 March 1973) and to request a submission for the *Tamarack Review*. He closes the letter as follows: "Incidentally, I am meeting a lady for coffee Thursday morning who is doing a piece about you for *Saturday Night* and I will try to be discreet" (MsC 37.2.8.10). The year 1973 marks the end of Munro's marriage. Alice partially moves out early in the year, and goes to the British Columbia interior to teach summer school and then back to Ontario in the fall.

Although Weaver's influence in Munro's career would seem to be pervasive, his is a rigorously professional mentorship, and her personal problems are somewhat out of his sphere. In his letter of 18 April 1973, Weaver appears to show a grudging willingness to help Munro make the break by agreeing to look into "the income tax business and get back to you right away" (MsC 37.2.8.11); the letter is addressed to the Munro household on Rockland Avenue in Victoria. The letter also refers to an earlier telephone conversation in which Munro asked about finding temporary accommodation in Toronto, for he says: "Naturally, as soon as we got off the phone the other day, I thought of a couple of places which might be able to provide you with a furnished apartment on a short term basis....If you like, I'd be glad to phone several places, or you may want to write or phone on your own. I will be glad to look around a little more if that would be helpful" (MsC 37.2.8.11). However, short-term real estate and marriage breakups are not Weaver's forte. Munro, as writer, may need a more personal mentorship, but she won't get that from Weaver, who quickly reverts to a more concrete offer of support, mentioning George Jonas's interest in a one-hour teleplay. Ever modest, he says "I have simply been arranging a preliminary approach in the case of a few writers, which is what I'm doing with you now" (MsC 37.2.8.11). Here, Weaver is as good as his word; the letter from Jonas is dated one week later, 25 April 1973.

By 18 September 1974, Weaver is writing to Munro at a London, Ontario, address; she has accepted a writer-in-residence position at Western. In his own way making it possible for her to remain independent, Weaver informs Munro in this letter that "Mordecai" thinks "it might be quite possible that Carleton would be prepared to have you as a writer-in-residence next winter" (MsC 37.2.8.13). He provides Richler's address as well. Two days later, Munro receives a letter from another CBC producer, Jeanine Locke, inviting her to participate in an interview series. Locke authorizes her approach by saying that "Robert Weaver, who gave me your address and telephone number, also gave his approval to the project that I'm writing you about" (MsC 37.2.8.14a). Locke concludes her offer by saying, "At our meeting, we can also discuss such coarse matters as money—we pay a very decent fee" (MsC 37.2.8.14a). It is precisely in the area of "such coarse matters as money" that Weaver can be most helpful to Munro; he may not be able to provide emotional or moral support as she attempts to break away from her marriage and achieve independence, but he can make sure that every opportunity to earn a living wage—a modest Canadian living wage, at least—is brought to her attention.

There are only two more letters in the Weaver file. The first, dated 21 June 1976, reaches Munro at a rural address in Clinton, where she is living with her soon-to-be second husband, Gerald Fremlin. The business part of the letter is about a revision of "Privilege" for *Anthology*; Weaver suggests changes which he invites Munro to either use or ignore. This is the first and only letter collected in Munro's archive which shows Weaver mentoring Munro in an editorial capacity. In all the other archival evidence, Weaver simply requests more material without any comment, positive or negative, on its quality. This is an important point because, according to Munro, her correspondence with Weaver included a fair amount of editorial advice and rejections. She says: "I would send him stories. He would buy them, or send them back. If he sent them back, there would always be a long letter telling me why. He never passed out judgments as anything final. He left me lots of room for disagreement, and was always ready to look at a story again, with changes I had made according to his criticisms or sometimes quite against them. Sometimes he would reconsider a story in which no changes had been made, and occasionally reverse an opinion, finding some power or grace in it he hadn't been able to see before" (Foreword ix).

This is the appropriate moment, then, to address an issue that has remained muted throughout my close reading of the Weaver correspondence: the issue of the incompleteness of the archival evidence. For example, why does the archive contain not a single "long letter" telling Munro why a story had been rejected? Why are there no rejection letters at all, no "criticisms"? Why were certain letters collected and others not? Are the omissions mere carelessness—the author not realizing the value of her papers and using a Weaver letter for a grocery list or a child's drawing, or simply tossing it in the garbage? Or are these absent letters absent by design? Did Munro *save* only certain kinds of letters, or did she *select* for the archive only the ones that deliberately construct a particular kind of narrative? In fact, Weaver did write several rejection letters to Munro, copies of which can be found in the Robert Weaver papers at the National Archives of Canada.[13] The method by which the archive comes to us is a mystery, and all we have is the material at hand, chosen or discarded by the author for reasons that can't be known. To go back to the *Dance of the Happy Shades* correspondence, for example, what if a flurry of letters went between Munro, Weaver, and Ryerson in the years between 1961 and 1967, but were somehow lost, discarded, or concealed? Would these letters explain that Ryerson had to indefinitely delay Munro's first book, owing to financial setbacks at the company, or personnel changes, or the hiring of an editor who disliked Munro's prose style? Would these hypothetical letters change in the mid-sixties, suggesting that the wave of cultural nationalism as Canada's centennial approached appeared to be making room for a book like *Dance of the Happy Shades*? On these questions I can only speculate.

As noted in the introduction, when I read a literary text, I do so without access to the author for explication, often with minimal biographical information and critical input. And I understand that the text before me presents not *the* truth but *a* truth, in which my close reading skills make me a participant in making meaning. An archive or manuscript collection is a fictional structure in its own right, a text in which the "author's" deletions, oversights, and emendations point to the construction of a particular kind of "story." The reason for the absence of Weaver's rejection letters from Munro's archive is unknown.

That said, I now return to the penultimate Weaver letter of 21 June 1976. After offering Munro editorial advice on a revision of "Privilege" for *Anthology*, the letter shifts to the personal:

> After I talked to you on Friday I told my wife that you certainly sounded very happy and as if your life and your writing are well under control. I hope this meant that you are going to turn into one of our most prolific, as well as one of our best writers. Incidentally, if you and your husband ever manage to come to Toronto together at some time when you could give me a few days warning, I'd like to have lunch with both of you. (MsC 37.2.8.15)

There's a tone of benediction in these words. Munro's personal, romantic, and emotional life is outside the range of Weaver's control and expertise. He is relieved to find her "life and...writing well under control" again after three tempestuous and transitory years; Munro is settling down to work again, so satisfactorily that Weaver (in the first reference to his own family in the collection) mentions the conversation to his wife. The mentor's blessing on the protege's new marital arrangements comes in the form of a lunch invitation.

Munro's correspondence with American literary agent Virginia Barber has begun by this time, and by November 1976 Munro has signed on with Barber. Her first *New Yorker* publication shortly follows. In 1974, Douglas Gibson at Macmillan offered Munro a publishing contract; by 1976, Gibson is pressing Munro for a "yes." (Munro eventually published *Who Do You Think You Are?* with Macmillan in 1978.) In short, as of June 1976, Munro's authority is increasing. She needs Weaver less now, and as Shirley Marchalonis points out in her introduction to *Patrons and Protegees*, "implicit in the concept of mentorship is the fact that the pupil must break away" (xiii).

The last letter in the Weaver file poignantly documents the changing relationship. Even the physical document is diminished. Instead of the usual typewritten letterhead, this last item is handwritten on a small piece of CBC memo paper. Weaver mentions the CBC Literary Competition, still guiding and suggesting opportunities for her. He also encloses a copy of *Books in Canada* in which he mentions Munro. The personal section of the letter describes a Robert Weaver who is *not* jetting off to New York or hobnobbing with publishers, but rather delivering the *Sunday Star* with his daughter. This is only the second time that his own family life is mentioned in the correspondence, indicating an equalizing shift in the quality of his relationship with Munro. As a result of this fatherly duty, Weaver says he has two extra copies of a *Star* profile about Munro, for which he was interviewed and which he encloses. He is uncharacteristically vague in his comment that: "I can't remember actually making the final quote attributed to me but never mind" (MsC 38.1.18.4). The letter is dated 7 May 1979. Munro has just won her second Governor General's Award, for *Who Do You Think You Are?* In this instance, Weaver did not serve on the jury, as he did with *Dance of the Happy Shades*.[14] In fact, although he has fostered her career, it has moved beyond him. Since the previous letter, Munro, working closely with Virginia Barber, has published in the *New Yorker*, has won the Canada-Australia Literary Prize, has published *The Beggar Maid* [15] in the United States, and has been shortlisted for the Booker Prize. When Munro makes her

move from Canadian petty-commodity publishing, with its government subsidy and academic bias, to the capitalist mode of
the United States, the mentorship of Robert Weaver becomes
less crucial to her authorial survival.

The opposition of the petty-commodity and capitalist modes
of publishing described by Davey is analogous in some ways to
Bourdieu's formulation of the two opposing fields of cultural
production: the field of restricted production, described as production for other producers, or "art for art's sake," and the field
of large-scale production, which produces art for the consumption of the public at large. Symbolic capital accrues to the
restricted producer as a result of her disavowal of economic
interest. In a small cultural milieu such as Canada, however, the
economic stakes are extremely limited, making the role of
restricted producer a financially precarious one. Davey notes
that, "unlike in other countries where national publishers operate on a similar scale to that of the country's bookstores, and
supply roughly 90% of the titles stocked by those stores, in
English Canada, national publishers have usually had access to
only 20% or less of bookstore sales" ("Writers" 90). This is a statistic of which Munro, as co-owner of a bookstore, must have
been aware. Her award-winning first book, *Dance of the Happy
Shades*, for example, received an initial print run of 2,500 copies.
Four years later, that initial print run had still not sold out.
Munro's American gambit is risky in terms of her symbolic capital as a restricted producer; however, her formative years as
restricted producer in the limited Canadian market play a large
role in her self-construction as author in the market capitalist
mode of American publishing, and Robert Weaver has played an
important role in creating the creator she is to become.

A mentor is defined in *Webster's New Twentieth Century
Dictionary* as "a wise and faithful counselor." However, certain
shifts in the material conditions of Munro's literary production
and in her position as author necessitate a different kind of
mentoring. Thus, her former mentor, wise and faithful certainly
within his Canadian area of power and expertise, closes his last
letter as follows: "I should have said something more to you at

the GG awards but everything seemed so overcrowded. Anyway, I'm sure you know how pleased I am" (MsC 38.1.18.4). In this benediction is the image of a proud father pushed to the sidelines at his daughter's glittering debut. Weaver's pride in Munro, however, is tempered by his suspicion, and possibly even resentment, of her new mentors. In a 1982 letter from the Barber Agency, Mary Evans asks Munro to forward a letter concerning copyright assignment to Robert Weaver, because Evans has found him reluctant or unwilling to respond to requests from the agency (Acc. 396/87.3 Box 2 File 3).[16]

Bourdieu's description of the "charismatic ideology" (*Field* 77) of literary creation describes quite accurately the way in which the figure of the "great publisher" Robert Weaver is viewed in Canadian culture. No doubt the (sometimes exaggerated and often self-mythologized) small size and relative newness of the Canadian cultural field, combined with government-supported cultural nationalism and the disproportionate influence of the academy all serve to naturalize this view. However, by the mid-seventies, when Munro crosses the line into what the cultural nationalists viewed as "the consumer-oriented mass society" (Buffie 234) of the United States, the contours of the playing field change dramatically.

## CHAPTER III

# "WOMAN"

# Useful Recognitions and Misrecognitions

The cultural field is an ideological structure, and, as Louis Althusser points out, "Ideology is a 'representation' of the imaginary relationship of individuals to their real conditions of existence" (52). Althusser adds that both recognition and misrecognition (*meconnaissance*) play a crucial role in "the reproduction of the relations of production and of the relations deriving from them" (57). In the correspondence between Alice Munro and Virginia Barber, recognition and misrecognition play equally important roles in the success of the author/agent relationship as it unfolds inside the ideological construction known as "literary culture."

On 11 March 1976, New York literary agent Virginia Barber writes to Alice Munro, offering to represent her.[1] The letter initiates a lengthy and fruitful working relationship and friendship. In moving beyond the confines of the Canadian market, Munro experiences a shift in the space of cultural production; in forming a business relationship with Virginia Barber, she engages in a struggle between her own image of her position in the literary field and that of her new cultural banker, who operates in a market capitalist literary economy unlike the petty-commodity marketplace of CanLit.

---

Notes for chapter 3 are on p. 173.

Furthermore, in such a pursuit of a wider authority, gender inevitably comes very much to the foreground. Because women are defined in language—a public language constructed by and for masculinist purposes in which the male is the norm and women's experience is "unintelligible, unreal, unfathomable" (Spender 2), claiming the status of "woman author" places one in a problematic, contradictory, conflicted position. It is in their mutual recognitions, their female friendship, that Barber and Munro find the resources to negotiate the misrecognitions that operate the cultural field.

In her discussion of poststructuralism, Chris Weedon notes that "language, far from reflecting an already given social reality, constitutes social reality for us" (22); thus "the meaning of [linguistic] signs is not intrinsic but relational" (23). She then expands on this concept to suggest that: "How we live our lives as conscious thinking subjects, and how we give meaning to the material social relations under which we live and which structure our everyday lives, depends on the range and social power of existing discourses, our access to them, and the political strength of the interests they represent" (26).

To be a woman is to be a person whose material social relations define her as subordinate, inferior, and often inexplicable. "Unfathomable" is a word that Munro gives Del Jordan to describe the lives of girls and women; critical studies of Munro's work bear such titles as Carrington's *Controlling the Uncontrol-lable* and Miller's *Saying the Unsayable.* Such descriptors reflect the contradictory positions of author ("control" and "say") and woman ("uncontrollable" as well as uncontrolling, and "unsay-able" as well as unsaying or silenced). Sharon Butala voices this sense of contradiction in her review of *Open Secrets:*

> With each book Munro's stories have grown longer, more complex, more detailed and subtle, and yet more fantastical. A friend says, "I want to like her stories, but they just seem crazy to me." There's a sense in which she's right. These stories are as profound a revelation of the female psyche as any written, and as such, without the key to their interpretation and

> with the expectation that they operate on the level most short
> stories do, they may well seem incomprehensible. (C16)

Butala acknowledges that, because they reveal "the female psyche," Munro's mature stories indeed seem "crazy" and "incomprehensible"—partly because crazy and incomprehensible
define "woman" under patriarchy. Beverly Rasporich extends
this idea to its stylistic implications: "If sexuality is for the
female contiguous and relative, then for Alice Munro as a female
author writing the body, fictional "novelistic" structures built on
correspondences and juxtapositions without ends and closure
are much more natural texts than the traditional narratives of
linear logic extended into climax" (162).

It is thus unsurprising that Munro's early work, before she
established her own authority, is generally less "crazy," more
"comprehensible," than the work of her later career. In her discussion of "Women and Writing" in *Man Made Language*, Dale
Spender notes how women writers "are doubly dependent on
men in that they depend upon the dominant group's evaluation
of their writing" (216), in addition to their dependence on men
for self-definition. This dependent or fatherly relationship, evident in the Weaver correspondence, shifts to a more "sisterly"
relationship in Munro's mid-career correspondence with Virginia
Barber. However, tensions and subtextual pressures related to
class, nationality, and genre are clearly legible, and the subjection of both agent and author to the demands of patriarchal literary ideology plays a significant role as well. Spender comments that "Women writers have always known—and still
know—that being evaluated by a woman is not of itself necessarily an advantage precisely because women have been
required to take on male definitions of themselves and the
world" (198).

To simply refute, step outside of, patriarchal authority is an
attractive idea, but as Chris Weedon points out in her discussion
of Althusser, such a step is not easily taken: "She [the individual]
speaks or thinks as if she were in control of meaning. She 'imag-
ines'...that she is indeed the type of subject which humanism

proposes—rational, unified, the source rather than the effect of language. It is the imaginary quality of the individual's identification with a subject position which gives it so much psychological and emotional force" (31). This imaginary quality, then, gives rise to the post-structuralist definition of human subjectivity as something "precarious, contradictory and in process, constantly being reconstituted in discourse each time we think or speak" (33). Weedon uses the example of consciousness-raising groups in the seventies as an example of how what were labelled "personal inadequacies or neuroses" can be redefined as "socially produced conflicts" (33) in a period of crisis and sociohistorical change. Thus, my references to Munro's "maturity" or her early career do not imply aesthetic value judgments, suggesting, for example, that Munro's later work is somehow "better" or that she has "progressed," but rather that these differences are part of an ongoing process of empowerment and resistance and authority, resulting from shifts in power relations as Munro's position in the cultural field changes. Weedon asserts that: "Discourses represent political interests and in consequence are constantly vying for status and power. The site of this battle for power is the subjectivity of the individual and it is a battle in which the individual is an active but not sovereign protagonist" (41). Discourses related to "Canadian-ness," gender, genre, and socio-economic position vie for status and power in Munro's struggle for authorship, a struggle in which she is an active but not sovereign protagonist.

An unpublished fragment collected in the Munro archive, titled "Certain Moments in Our History," illustrates the point. This fragment details the thoughts of a woman writer named Donna, who is on the verge of leaving her husband. Donna (the Spanish word for "lady" or "woman") ponders what she has left out of her fictions: two examples are a childhood sexual assault by a group of boys, and physical abuse by her father. Donna's subject position as a woman does not allow her as author to speak openly about such abuses. Yet a paragraph later, Donna berates herself for trivializing the truth of her experience by writing about it. In the role of author, she has commodified her own history; however, as a woman about to leave the economic security of marriage, she has to make a living somehow. She's in a no-win situation; she can neither tell the whole truth of her experience, nor can she avoid a sense of shame at telling what she is permitted to tell (MsC 37.14.27). The "shyness"[2] and "modesty" ascribed to Munro is explained by the author herself as the result of "being a woman of a certain generation" ("Writing's Something I Did" E1), and certainly her generation plays a role in this self-construction, but another large part of this bind results from the antithetical roles of "author" and "woman" in contemporary literary culture.

Interestingly, the materials of this fragment known as "Certain Moments in Our History" do evolve into a published story, with the two passages mentioned omitted. (Munro is an inveterate recycler.) The story is "Providence," from *Who Do You Think You Are?*, in which Rose leaves her husband Patrick for an independent life as a broadcaster in a small British Columbia town. The narrative of the story shows the impossibility of reconciling motherhood, career, and a lover. By the story's end, Rose has lost both child and lover. Only her low-paid job and a tenuous pride in her independence remain. As Sidonie Smith suggests in her chapter on "Autobiographical Criticism and the Problematics of Gender," rugged individualism is a male script; for a woman, however, "rebellious pursuit is potentially catastrophic," and to "call attention to her distinctiveness is to become 'unfeminine'" (9). Munro's story reflects this by showing how Rose's bid for independence brings on a spate of blizzards, mechanical breakdowns, and viruses—in short, catastrophe.

In current theorization, then, an author works with language—in a sense "owns" language—and a woman is defined in language. To authorize different language uses, a woman writer therefore struggles with her lack of proprietary rights. Certainly, Munro's published work struggles with ideological assumptions about gender and authority. Characters like Del Jordan and Rose, like the central characters in "Dulse" and "Postcard," walk off into the sunset alone. However, the narrative action of the stories centres

on the characters' desire for the seemingly unachievable happy
ending, and the given ending has an aspect of grudging compromise; it is as if the character were deciding that if she can't have
it all (usually meaning the power of the male as well as the privileges of the female, such as motherhood, marriage, sexual attractiveness), then she'll have to settle for selfhood, art, or independence. Early on in her career, Munro says that the "twin
choices of my life...were marriage and motherhood, or the black
life of the artist" (Tausky x). The conflict between the discourse
of marriage and motherhood (selflessness, submission, woman)
and authorship (selfishness, power, man) recurs throughout her
work and in her archive. If, as many critics suggest, Munro's published work wrestles with the question of female power, her
archive is a site where the conflict between gender and authority
is very much in evidence. It is in the archive that I witness the
"conflicted psyche of an achieving woman" (Buss, *Mapping* 126)
as I observe the struggle of Munro the woman to become Munro
the author, striving to take on the proprietary linguistic powers
of the author function when her materials, her life experience,
her very self, is subject to the subordinating power of what Dale
Spender calls "man made language."

In the Barber correspondence, the author as writing subject in
culture is visible in a gradual but necessarily incomplete process
of empowerment. Or, in Chris Weedon's terms, she is visible as
"an active but not sovereign protagonist" (41) in a power struggle. Munro is undertaking to expand her authority to the
American market, and Barber herself, as Munro comments in her
1996 *Morningside* interview, was "just starting out too." Both
women act out their efforts of self-empowerment inside a patri-
archally defined cultural field. The correspondence contains evidence of the power struggle that occurs when women attempt to
combine business with friendship. In a *Publisher's Weekly* article,
Beverley Slopen describes the mid-seventies as a time when
Munro's life took "two unexpected turns" (77). Munro's marriage
ended in 1973, and she returned to Ontario with her youngest
daughter. The first "unexpected turn" was that Munro re-
encountered a former Western classmate, geographer Gerald

Fremlin; she subsequently married Fremlin and moved to Clinton, less than thirty miles from Wingham, the town where she had been born and raised.

The other unexpected turn, according to Slopen, was that after the Canadian publication of *Something I've Been Meaning to Tell You* in 1974, Munro received "a letter from US literary agent Virgina Barber asking to represent her. Feeling that she did not have enough material to offer, Munro replied diffidently, but subsequently she sent Barber some stories. The agent immediately sold two of them to the *New Yorker*, and made arrangements with Knopf to publish Munro's future works" (77). Slopen's version of Munro's authorial story is undercut, or at the very least complicated, by the evidence of the archive, which shows that the process of empowerment and authority of the period was aided by the sisterhood of Barber, but compromised and challenged by the ideological structures of the cultural field. In effect, this particular "unexpected turn" is far less accidental and more ideologically grounded than Slopen's comment takes into account.

Slopen suggests that Barber's initial contact with Munro occurred in 1974, but Barber's first approach must have been indirect or verbal, because the letter mentioned above is dated March 1976, and it has the flavour of a first direct contact between the two women. After presenting her qualifications for the position of agent, Barber praises Munro's work, particularly the story "Material," in which the narrator questions the authority of a male writer, her husband Hugo, to make people and events "pass...into art" in the creative act, an act of "special, unsparing, unsentimental love" ("Material" 35). The word "authority" is crucial. Part of what Barber admires about "Material" is the way it questions a literary ideology that rewards cleverness and stylish trickery but overlooks or ignores the mundane realities of individual lives. It would appear that Barber reads a feminist subtext in the story, and the contract in which she hopes to engage Munro has as one its projects (aside from earning a living) defining what a female literary authority might look like.

Barber's next letter is dated just eleven days later. Though the tone is somewhat warmer, the bulk of the letter is brisk and businesslike, attending to every detail of commission, sales, publishing, contracts, promotion, and copyright. Though the letter ends in a lighthearted personal tone, it's clear that Barber is a knowledgeable professional.

The stark contrast between the tenor of the Barber correspondence and that of the Weaver letters is obvious. For one thing, Barber discusses foreign sales with conviction, as if such sales were a reasonable expectation rather than a remote possibility, whereas Weaver's response to Munro's American ambitions was far more tentative (MsC 37.2.8.7). There is in Barber's voice less the tone of the supplicant than the assurance of a businesswoman. According to Pierre Bourdieu, "Although dealers form a protective screen between the artist and the market, they are also what link them to the market, and so provoke, by their very existence, cruel unmaskings of the truth of artistic practice"(*Field* 79). Thus, while in Barber's first letter the connection is personal, and Barber addresses Munro as one who understands and supports her work, the second letter unmasks the underlying economics of the author/agent relationship, and it is possibly for this reason that Munro takes six months to think things over before signing on.

In two letters sent while Munro is still deciding whether to sign on with the Barber Agency, Barber reiterates her eagerness to read some new work, and urges Munro to send some stories as soon as possible. The letters end with a jokey, woman-to-woman tone, in which Barber appears to be reforging the personal connection, the connection of two women interested in the relationship between art and women's lives. Bourdieu characterizes author and literary marketer as "*adversaries in collusion* who each abide by the same law which demands the repression of direct manifestations of personal interest, at least in its overtly 'economic' form" (79). The Munro/Barber partnership unfolds in this vein of aesthetic association and friendship, which masks the underlying exigencies of profit and loss.

Once Munro does decide to send her stories to Barber, how-ever, good things begin to happen very quickly. The deal is clinched when, on 18 November, just one week after Barber receives the stories which Munro has finally decided to send, Charles (Chip) McGrath at the *New Yorker* writes to Munro: "Your story 'Royal Beatings' has occasioned as much excitement around here as any story I can remember. It's an extraordinary, original piece of writing, and we very much want to publish it. Everyone who has read it has been moved by the story's intelli-gence and sensitivity, and has marvelled at its emotional range" (MsC 37.2.30.1a).

McGrath's letter is doubtless sweet vindication for an author who tried to publish in the *New Yorker* more than twenty years before. It must have seemed to Munro that Barber was capable of working miracles, especially in light of the extremely short time frame: less than a month has passed since Munro sent the stories. If Munro wasn't certain that she really needed an agent before, she must have been soundly convinced of that need at this point.

Publication in the *New Yorker* authorizes Munro in a far dif-ferent—broader, more lucrative, more symbolically powerful—cultural field than she is accustomed to and thus, ironically, but not surprisingly, it is also a moment at which Munro senses the conflict between identity as author and identity as woman keenly. On 17 November 1976, Barber writes to Munro—the day of McGrath's letter of acceptance to Barber, and the day before he writes the good news to Munro. On the back of this letter is a doodle, described in the archive catalogue as "A. Munro's holo-graph annotation on verso." Various names, phone numbers and reminders are scribbled here, but one which catches the eye is the name "Alice Fremlin." It would appear that Munro, in this idle scribbling, probably done while talking on the telephone, is trying on her "new" name. (Munro married Gerald Fremlin in 1976.) The juxtaposition of *New Yorker* negotiations with this schoolgirl's game is intriguing: while Munro the author is "mak-ing a name" for herself in her new associations with Virginia Barber and the *New Yorker,* at the same time she is making a new name for herself as woman, lover, wife.

However, the conflict between these two "names" is elaborated powerfully on the back of another letter from Virginia Barber dating from the same period as the one just mentioned[3] (37.2.47.1). Though only the second page of this letter is extant, it shows how Barber is also in the position of "making a name" for herself, when she asks Munro to mention her name to up-and-coming Canadian writers in need of an agent. Ironically, Munro's holograph annotations on the back of this document repeat the previous name-game, with some fascinating variations. The name "Alice Munro" appears twice. At right angles to that is the name "Alice Fremlin," also repeated, the second time enclosed in a cloud. On turning the page upside down, one sees yet another name repeated, with variable spelling: Jelly Flemin, Gelly Flemlin.

The names of the author, the wife, and the lover/husband thus contend with each other, possibly because, at this point, Munro is claiming the masculine power of the author function. Munro's perception of the conflicts of female authorship is evident in an interview with Alan Twigg in the 1981 *For Openers:*

> I think it's still possible for men in public to be outrageous in ways that it's not possible for women to be. It still seems to be true that no matter what a man does, there are women who will be in love with him. It's not true the other way round. I think achievement and ability are positively attractive qualities in men that will overcome all kinds of behavior and looks, but I don't think the same is true for women.
>
> A falling-down-drunk poet may have great power because he has talent. But I don't think men are attracted to women for these reasons. If they are attracted to talent, it has to be combined with the traditionally attractive female qualities. If a woman comes on shouting and drinking, she won't be forgiven. (20)

In this passage are evident many of the perceptions of the ideological tension in Munro's two subject positions—that of author and that of woman. Whereas a man's authority adds to his attractiveness, a woman who receives offers from the *New Yorker* is in a dangerous position, in danger of not being "forgiven" for her power, of forfeiting her "traditionally attractive female qualities"—in short, of going through life unloved. Munro's idle doodlings on the back of a business letter attest to the psychic conflict; they show Munro unconsciously recognizing the bind in which her gender places her as an author.

It is not on the question of gender alone that ideological tensions are evident in the Barber correspondence, however. As the relationship establishes itself, issues of genre, nationality, and economics intertwine with the tensions between gender and authority.

Genre bias begins to complicate the picture within a year of Barber's initial contact with Munro. At first, Barber claims a disinterestedness in terms of genre preference and appears to merely echo the position of previous editors that, if you possibly can, it's best to bring out a novel before a short story collection. However, at this early stage, and considering her success with marketing Munro's stories, the pressure at this point is fairly low. But as time goes on, the pressure increases, and Barber begins to push, subtly and cautiously, for a novel (e.g., MsC. 37.2.47.3, 5, 6).

As Dale Spender points out, any woman who holds a position of power in literary culture, whether author, editor, or agent, is handicapped by a lifetime indoctrination into the literary ideology of the dominant culture, and a familiar refrain of the publishing world is that novels are better than stories, because, among other things, they are more marketable. This is one of many points of contrast between the Robert Weaver and Virginia Barber mentorships: Weaver's position in a small, government-subsidized market allows him to encourage Munro to "continue on in the short story" for now, and to ignore "the novel problem" (MsC 37.2.8.8); for Barber, however, the pressures of the mass market are much more urgent. Barber's concerns over genre are indicative of her position inside mainstream culture, a culture in which the short story is a lesser genre, possibly even a "female" genre, and probably a "Canadian" one as well. The subtlety of Barber's approach on this matter indicates the delicacy of their mutual misrecognitions.

The function of intermediary is evident also in Barber's deal-
ings with rejection letters. If, as Bourdieu suggests, part of the
cultural businessperson's equivocal role is to act as buffer
between the artist and the harsh realities of the marketplace, this
is certainly evident in the way Barber steps in to mediate the blow
of a *New Yorker* rejection from Charles McGrath. McGrath rejects
"Mischief" in a 1977 letter to Barber, saying: "In many ways this
is the best written and most polished of all the Munro stories you
sent us, but it's also the most familiar in subject*, and most people who read it here felt that it was simply too long" (MsC
37.2.47.6b). On the copy of the McGrath letter that Barber for-
wards to Munro, Barber places an asterisk at the words "familiar
in subject" (which are a chilling echo of Munro's early *New Yorker*
rejections of the fifties, with their mention of her "overly familiar" themes) and adds a handwritten note expressing her disagreement with McGrath's assessment. Barber, now signing off
with her nickname, thus tempers, with an offer of female soli-
darity, a rejection which appears to suggest that there is nothing
new in a woman's treatment of an old subject. Interestingly, the
story was also rejected by Gordon Lish at *Esquire* for similar reasons: he says that the narrator's "escape from that assignation
[Rose's failed attempt at an affair with Clifford]...is elided," that
the flashbacks need "more graceful movement" or to be cut, and
that Munro should "cut the last line after 'oldest friends she had.'
[Because] What follows is too cute" (MsC 37.2.47.11). The "cute"
line referred to by Lish is Rose's cynical decision to remain
friends with Clifford and Jocelyn, despite their betrayal, "because
she needed such friends occasionally, at that stage of her life"
(135). It would seem that Lish is asking for a more traditional
adultery story: more sex and less speculation, historicization,
and cynicism. The story was eventually published in *Viva*, a magazine of erotica for women, in April 1978.

Although Munro is able to rely on Barber's support and comfort
in the face of the rejection, in the months leading up to the problematic publication of *Who Do You Think You Are?* and beyond,
the road becomes rougher. There are rejections and disappoint-
ments and some very costly problems with publishing rights.

Beverley Slopen's article says that Barber, in addition to securing the first *New Yorker* publications, also quickly got Munro a publishing contract with Knopf. In fact, *Who Do You Think You Are?*, published in the U.S. as *The Beggar Maid*, went first to Norton, whose editor Sherry Huber did her best to make the book into a novel. The Norton contract eventually fell through in the fall of 1978, when the Canadian edition was about to go to press. Huber's employment with Norton ended at the same time, though whether Huber's struggle to transform Munro's story sequence into a novel was a factor is unknown. It was only then that Alfred A. Knopf picked up the book and began Munro's association with Knopf editor Ann Close. Thus, the securing of an American publisher was a more complicated process than Slopen's article indicates, and it attests to the hard work of women like Barber, Huber, and Close in making Munro "respectable" enough by market standards to make this breakthrough.

In the winter of 1978, a period of intense struggle over the ultimate form of *Who Do You Think You Are?*, discussed in detail in chapter 4, a six-month gap occurs in the collected Barber correspondence, though this gap may be merely an omission, either accidental or deliberate. Thus, Barber's role in this particular episode is not documented. However, Spender's remark on the indoctrination of literary women to the ideology of a patriarchal literary culture provides a useful reminder of what Barber's position must have been: "Patriarchy is an interlocking system with its psychological and material components, and while women's consciousness may indicate the desirability and even necessity of practising 'disagreeableness' in order to undermine patriarchy, material circumstances may prevent them from doing so" (4). Thus, though Barber applauds Munro's "disagreeableness" in psychological terms (e.g., the questioning of male literary authority), in material terms she is required to prompt Munro to produce a book that will sell. It is in June 1978 that Munro's generic difficulties with the form of *Who Do You Think You Are?* reach a crisis point and the pressure from her American publishers to make the short story collection into a novel is intense. At this juncture, Barber's equivocal position

would be at the forefront, and, as Bourdieu points out concerning cultural businesspeople, there is a "need to possess, simultaneously, economic dispositions which, in some sectors of the
field, are totally alien to the producers and also properties close
to those of the producers whose work they valorize and exploit"
(*Field* 39). In short, the "adversaries in collusion" construction of
the author-agent relationship may create problems for both
women at various points in their association.

If genre bias begins to reveal itself as a problem, Munro's
nationality is also seen as a handicap to be overcome. Like her
gender, Munro's Canadian-ness is something that must be sup-
pressed in order for her to achieve authority. For example,
Barber confesses to disappointment at being unable to find an
American publisher for one of Munro's stories and grudgingly
sends "Working for a Living" to the Canadian literary journal
*Tamarack Review*, only as a last resort (MsC 38.2.63.52). Yet
Barber is also sensitive to Munro's status as a Canadian. When
two publishers, one in Quebec and one in France, propose translations of her books, Barber asks whether nationalism is an issue
for Munro. The translations are ultimately published by the
French-Canadian company (MsC 38.2.63.25), but whether the
choice is nationalistic or practical is unknown.

The publication of *Who Do You Think You Are?* presents several instances in which the ideological and practical differences
between the American literary marketplace and the Canadian
one were painfully evident. The most obvious is Knopf's insistence on changing the title of the book to *The Beggar Maid*.
Munro says that the American publishers "felt the colloquial
put-down [who do you think you are?] was not familiar to most
Americans. I had to accept that, though I think it probably is in
certain parts of the U.S. anyway" (Struthers, "Real" 29). Munro's
editor at Knopf addresses the problem of title in a letter of
19 January 1979 (MsC. 38.1.3.6a). The letter establishes its authority by naming the group of experts who are "here," meaning
America, as opposed to "there," meaning the far different cultural
space known as Canada. The choice of the title of "Beggar Maid"
could be seen as an ironic statement of Munro's position in the

American culture she attempts to enter with the publication of this book. The American title is decidedly less impudent than the Canadian one, and in Close's determination to showcase Munro's writerly talents over her nationality lies the slightest suggestion that these two aspects might be antithetical. In another sense, the reprimand "who do you think you are?" relates to a distaste for "showing off," which Munro sees as "rather Canadian" (Wachtel 104). The wrangling over the book's title provides an image of the differences between the Canadian and American literary markets; unlike Canadians, who are in the process of building a national literature, Americans already know *exactly* who they are.

Aside from nationality and genre, a crucial issue that surfaces in the Barber-Munro correspondence is that of the fiduciary nature of the relationship between author and agent. Barber's letter of introduction in 1976 enumerated her qualifications, including a doctorate from Duke and a husband active in the publishing business. The Greenwich Avenue, New York, address on her letterhead certainly added credibility, and Barber quickly demonstrated her powerful connections in the early months of her association with Munro, by quickly securing the author her first *New Yorker* publication.

Certainly, it is beyond dispute that Munro's work is permeated with an acute awareness of class differences. In the story "The Beggar Maid," for example, Rose decides to marry Patrick after all, partly because "only middle class people had choices anyway" (97). In an interview with the *Paris Review* in 1994, Munro commented that, in her early years as a writer, "I didn't realize that women didn't become writers as readily as men, and that neither did people from a lower class" (McCulloch and Simpson 257). This characterization of herself as a person from the lower classes is evident in her accounts of her first marriage as well. She describes her in-laws as being doubtful of her suitability as a wife for Jim Munro, partly because of her "lower caste" and her lack of "breeding" (qtd. in C. Ross 49). Munro says that, when she met her first husband, she had "never known people of this class before" (McCulloch and Simpson 247), and she bristled at the fact that "Life was very tightly managed as a series of permitted recreations, permitted opinions and permitted ways of being a woman....I'd meet a university professor or someone, and if I knew something about what he knew, that would not be considered acceptable conversation" (252).

Barber and Munro had in common their interest in art and women's lives, and both had been bright, ambitious young women who had grown up in parochial small-town environments (Munro in southwestern Ontario, Barber in the Blue Ridge mountains of Virginia). Their bond is reflected in personal information exchanged in letters, in jokes about children, and in Barber's signing off with "Love, Ginger." (In the Weaver correspondence, which covers more than twenty years, there is not a single letter signed "Love, Bob.") On the other hand, as literary agent, as "cultural banker" (Bourdieu 75), Barber was one of "these 'merchants in the temple' [who] make their living by tricking the artist or writer into taking the consequences of his or her statutory professions of disinterestedness" (40), for "only those who can come to terms with the 'economic' constraints inscribed in this bad-faith economy can reap the full 'economic' profits of their symbolic capital" (76). James L. West III, in *American Authors and the Literary Marketplace since 1900*, explains the dilemma in simpler but equally useful terms when he points out that an author is neither "professional" nor "tradesman" but a pieceworker who must enter into a fiduciary relationship with the quasi-professional classes of publishers and agents in order to find an audience and earn a living (20).

According to West, "authors were left behind when the American middle class professionalized itself, and the business conditions under which they have worked since 1900 have been anachronistic" (20). He adds that "authorship in America has not been a profession during this century, nor has it been a trade. It has been more nearly a craft, a cottage industry. The author has crafted literary piecework at home and has carried it to the publisher, who has turned it into salable goods" (20). Like any day labourer, Munro is dependent on her agent and her publisher for marketing the goods that she produces. However, just as Barber must allow Munro her "shyness" and "modesty"—crucial aspects of her self-construction as a serious artist—Munro must likewise allow Barber her commissions in exchange for her professional handling of the products of Munro's "cottage industry."

For Munro and Barber, the tensions of their business relationship are mitigated by a strong foundation of sisterhood and friendship—a recognition of mutual ground that helps to diffuse, if not defeat, the exigencies of the literary marketplace. *Selected Stories* is a retrospective of Munro's career, a selection of stories from the early years to 1996. The dedication page reads:

> For Virginia Barber
> my essential support and
> friend for twenty years

These words attest to the fact that, whatever the tensions and ruptures in their relationship, Munro still acknowledges Barber as a friend in this summation of her career. But even more important is Munro's acknowledgement of how "essential" the "support" of this cultural banker has been to the formation of her authority. In the 1996 *Morningside* interview, Munro remarked of Barber, "She got me into the *New Yorker*," to which Peter Gzowski replied, "No, Ms Munro, you got yourself into the *New Yorker*." More likely, the joint efforts of author and agent can be credited with achieving that particular step toward the fullness of the author function. Barber and Munro have "recognized" each other as women friends, but they have also "misrecognized" their author-agent relationship to their mutual benefit.

## CHAPTER IV

# "SHORT STORY"
## Remaking Genre

In a 1994 *Morningside* interview, Peter Gzowski credits Munro with reinventing the short story form with the dense, complex stories of *Open Secrets*. Critic Oakland Ross also suggests that she has transformed the cultural economy as well; Ross begins his review of *Strangers Are Like Children*, by Joan Baxter, as follows: "It's a sad truth of the literary marketplace in Canada that short-story collections don't sell, unless they are written by Alice Munro" (C8). If Munro has reinvented the genre and transformed the market, this feat is certainly due in part to her great gift and her persistence in cultivating it, but the achievement is also the result of long-term resistance to the more constricting rules of the field. Munro's nationality and gender certainly complicate her pursuit of authorship, but it is on the question of genre that Munro's formation as a writing subject meets its greatest challenges.

What is the actual status of the short story within the literary culture(s) where Munro seeks authority? On the one hand, Canada's burgeoning literary scene makes the genre reasonably lucrative, and the consecrating powers of the CBC and the literary magazines are considerable. On the other hand, the audience in such venues is (in the imagination of the artistic com-

---

Notes for chapter 4 are on pp. 173-74.

munity, if not in fact) so small that the producer/editor knows all of his listeners/subscribers by name. Likewise, in the United States, venues like the *New Yorker* or *McCall's* are rewarding both symbolically and financially. However, magazine pieces don't have the shelf life of books, and they rarely receive what Robert Lecker calls "the value conferred by prize-giving or other forms of certification" ("Anthologizing" 57). Anthology publication is a more durable venue, and a good means of academic exposure, but the financial rewards are mediocre. Finally, though the short story is Munro's genre, book publishers on both sides of the border are reluctant to publish a short story collection for market reasons. To reap the rewards of all three of these markets—magazine, anthology, and published collection—is, in a way, to "have it all," as a rather trite feminist slogan used to promise. Munro's choice of the marginalized but, in Canada at least, relatively marketable genre is severely tested in the years between 1976 and 1978, but she rises to the challenge magnificently in the production of her fourth book.

In "The Short Story: An Underrated Art," Thomas Gullason mentions Gustav Flaubert's *Madame Bovary* as the "impetus" for the privileging of the novel in the literary hierarchy of genres (13). Bourdieu, likewise, finds Flaubert's influence extremely significant, and his analysis of how the work of Flaubert changed the form of the novel in France provides a useful analogy to Munro's situation. Bourdieu observes:

> When Flaubert undertook to write *Madame Bovary* or *Sentimental Education*, he situated himself actively within the space of possiblities offered by the field….In choosing to write these novels, Flaubert risked the inferior status associated with a minor genre. Above all, he condemned himself to take a place within a space that was already staked out with names of authors, names of sub-genres (the historical novel, the serial, and so on) and names of movements or schools (realism). Despite Balzac's prestige, the novel was indeed perceived as an inferior genre. (*Field* 203)

If one applied Bourdieu's analysis of a French nineteenth-century male novelist to our twentieth-century Canadian woman short story author, the analogy holds. For example, in choosing to write a book like *Who Do You Think You Are?*, Munro actively situates herself in the space of possibilities offered by the field; she attempts to produce a "story sequence," which appears to be one of the less desirable options available within "the universe of possible choices" (203). She risks "inferior status" because of her association with the "minor genre" of the short story, yet she also "condemns" herself to take a place in a space already staked out by authors such as Anne Tyler, whose novels are both literary and profitable, and a space structured by the subgenre of the modern "literary" (as opposed to "magazine") short story, as well as by the movement or school of "realism."

Pierre Bourdieu's concept of "habitus" provides a useful approach to understanding Munro's position in the cultural field. Bourdieu defines "habitus" as constituted by "schemes of perception and appreciation," as a "sense of social direction." The relationship between the habitus and the field is the result of

> the configuration, at the moment, and at the various critical turning points in each career, of the space of available possibilities (in particular, the economic and symbolic hierarchy of the genres, schools, styles, manners, subjects, etc.), the social value attached to each of them, and also the meaning and value they received for the different agents or classes of agents in terms of the socially constituted categories of perception and appreciation they applied to them. (*Field* 65)

Bourdieu shows how Flaubert, by virtue of his sociohistoricity and habitus was "predisposed...to experience at their strongest the force of contradictions inscribed in the position of the writer and in the position of the pure artist, where these contradictions attained their highest degree of intensity" (202). By "writer," Bourdieu refers to the artist in the marketplace, and by "pure artist" to the producer in the field of restricted production, that of "art for art's sake"; in short, he is saying that Flaubert found himself in the contradictory space between the real and the ideological.

Bourdieu suggests that Flaubert reinvented the novel, and that "what confers on his work an incomparable *value*, is his relationship, albeit negative, with the whole literary world in which he acted and whose contradictions and problems he assumed absolutely" (205). In a 1994 *Morningside* interview following the publication of *Open Secrets*, Peter Gzowski suggests that Munro has, with this new collection, reinvented the short story, "a new form that is between novel and short story...not novella but...in fact a short novel." However, the defensiveness of Munro's response to Gzowski's praise indicates how she "assumes absolutely" these "contradictions and problems": she says, "You mean, I could've written eight novels if I'd just set my mind to it?". The remark echoes Bourdieu's observation that "the whole time he was working on *Madame Bovary*, Flaubert never stopped talking about his suffering, even his despair... above all, he repeated over and over again that he did not, strictly speaking, know what he was doing" (204-205).

The history of the production of Munro's fourth book, *Who Do You Think You Are?*, is a complicated one. When the Canadian version of the book was in galleys, Munro made drastic changes to the structure of the text, at her own expense, transforming it from a metafictional short story collection to a "story sequence" about a single character. In an interview with Tim Struthers, Munro explains the difficulties, negotiations, and last-minute changes in terms of her own "stupidity." She says it was "not a question of me being persuaded against my will. It's just a question of me being too stupid to see, or being not clear about what I would do next" (Struthers, "Real" 31). What Munro did do next, after this ideological struggle over the hierarchy of genres, was first to establish her own position by refusing to produce any more collections of linked stories, and second to reinvent the short story with each succeeding book, until by the time she produces *Open Secrets*, her transformation of the genre is acknowledged. It is this moment of intense struggle in the final arrangment of the stories in *Who Do You Think You Are?/The Beggar Maid* that shows Munro's most ambiguous, troubled, but very powerful negotiation with the construct of literary authorship.

In his discussion of the "hierarchy of genres," Pierre Bourdieu does not mention the short story. He does, however, situate the novel in the hierarchy with some implications that are useful to this discussion. Bourdieu differentiates two points of view in the hierarchization of the literary field. From the economic point of view, drama is at the top, poetry at the bottom. The novel he places in between, because it

> can secure big profits (in the case of some naturalist novels), and sometimes very big profits (some "popular" novels), for a relatively large number of producers, from an audience which may extend far beyond the audience made up of the writers themselves, as in the case of poetry, and beyond the bourgeois audience, as in the case of theatre, into the *petite bourgeoisie* or even, especially through municipal libraries, into the "labour aristocracy." (*Field* 48)

Thus the novel is a form whose profitability results from the breadth of its potential audience, which ranges from what Bourdieu has described earlier as "the field of restricted production," or production for other producers (and certainly the designation "a writers' writer" is often applied to Munro[1]), through the *bourgeois* and even including some members of the working class. However, according to Bourdieu, the hierarchy is reversed when one takes the symbolic point of view. Because the disavowal or repression of the economic increases symbolic capital, then poetry takes its place at the top of the symbolic hierarchy because of its small audience and its unprofitability, while drama (and film, in our century), with its larger audiences and larger profits, is at the bottom of the pile. The case for the novel, however, is more complex, because "the hierarchy of specialties"—that is, "the degree to which the authors and works conform to the specific demands of the genre"—"corresponds to the hierarchy of the audiences reached and also, fairly strictly, to the hierarchy of the social universes represented" (*Field* 48). The difference between a "literary" novel and a "bestseller" is a matter of subgenre, or "specialties." Certain features distinguish serious fiction, such as a tendency to prevalently anti-bourgeois attitudes, the "literary" use of language, metaphor, and symbol, as well as inclusion on academic syllabuses and attention from serious critical venues. Literary fiction does "cross over" in some cases, but a serious work that achieves commercial success risks being judged as "popular" or "commercial." In short, the smaller the audience and the lower the profits, the more "autonomy" the author supposedly enjoys, and thus the more symbolic capital inheres to his/her work.

The omission of the short story in Bourdieu's discussion of genre hierarchies is unsurprising. The neglect of the short story in literary criticism and theory has been noted by a variety of scholars. For example, in a collection of essays called *Short Story Theories*, editor Charles E. May asserts that, "Compared with the vast amount of theoretical criticism on the novel, serious approaches to the short story have been embarrassingly few" (xi). Likewise, in *Re-Reading the Short Story*, Clare Hanson remarks that "For a complex of reasons the short story has been largely excluded from the arena of contemporary critical debate" (1). The reasons for this neglect can be attributed to three factors. First, the short story has had a briefer history, as a literary form, than the novel, and thus has simply not had the time to achieve critical respect. Second, the short story is more "popular" than the novel, because of its marketability in magazines, and thus is deemed less worthy by critics, which is in accord with Bourdieu's view of the hierarchy of genres and the field of production. Third, the formal properties of the novel more closely inscribe the ideology of the dominant culture, thus making it a more central form.

In terms of its history, the short story is a twentieth-century phenomenon in the sense that serious critical and academic attention to the form is a relatively recent development, far more recent than for drama, poetry, and even the novel. North American short story theory begins with Poe's review of Hawthorne's *Twice-Told Tales* in 1842, in which the critic insists on the importance of "unity of effect or impression" (47). In 1901, Brander Matthews reiterates and expands upon Poe's ideas in his essay "The Philosophy of the Short Story," asserting that "The difference in spirit and in form between the Lyric and the Epic is scarcely greater than the difference between the Short-story and the Novel" (53), thus beginning a long line of defensive postures vis-à-vis the relative merits of the two genres. The modernist challenge to the realist model of Poe and Matthews is evident by the postwar period, and is detailed in A.L. Bader's "The Structure of the Modern Short Story" (1945). Frank Davey asserts that the short story achieved academic acceptance in the postwar period not only because of the work of short story theorists and critics, but also for the very practical reason that it upheld the ideology of the current theoretical orthodoxy, namely the New Criticism. Following his survey of critics such as Poe, Matthews, and Bader, Davey suggests that: "An even stronger attempt to establish the unity of the short story, and to valorize the story as an object of high art, was made by the New Critics, who used it, along with the lyric poem, as a pedagogical tool in the attempt to teach literature and taste to the newly large and democratized freshman classes that came to U.S. universities following the Second World War" ("Writers" 139). Certainly, the short story would appear an ideal vehicle for the New Critical ideology of the "well-wrought urn," and it is an accessible form, pedagogically. This rise of the short story anthology in both the United States and Canada parallels the postwar democratization of the university. As Bourdieu remarks, "economic and social changes affect the literary field indirectly, through the growth in the cultivated audience, i.e. the potential readership, which is itself linked to increased schooling" (*Field* 54).

If the critical history of the short story and of short story criticism in the United States is brief, in Canada it is even briefer. When Robert Weaver published the World's Classics Series *Canadian Short Stories* in 1960, he asserted that "there have been so few collections of Canadian short stories that there is no tradition which an editor must either follow or explain away" (ix). In fact, there had been several anthologies published before this,[2] but the 1960 publication is regarded as a watershed by most Canadian literary historians. The work is a historical survey of sorts, including stories by Roberts, Haliburton, and Leacock, but Weaver states quite bluntly that few stories of merit, by his standards, were produced in Canada before 1920.

Weaver's introduction to the collection concludes with a kind of
apology, an admission that the stories which follow might be
read as lacking in sophistication, as "naive"—a situation that
Weaver hopes to see change, and that, indeed, he plays a key role
in changing.[3]

In her discussion of canon and genre in Robert Lecker's
*Canadian Canons*, Donna Bennett sees two historical factors
that helped to establish the short story genre in Canada in the
mid-twentieth century. First, she observes that poetry was the
most prestigious genre until the mid-1960s after which "prose
fiction [was seen] as the central form of contemporary literature" (136). Secondly, notes Bennett, "investment in radio and
television broadcasting has greatly increased the importance of
the short story as a canonical form, for writers can gain exposure as well as money by working in this genre. (In contrast,
book publication privileges the novel as the only important literary form for financial return.)" (147). For Munro, at least in
Canada, the privileging of the novel over the short story is partly
mitigated by the short story's academic acceptance, its marketability to the public broadcasting service, and the relative
youth of the Canadian literary culture as a whole.

The second factor in the depriviliging of the short story genre
in literary culture is its "popular" appeal. As Bourdieu points out,
there is an inverse relationship, in the literary field, between popular success and literary seriousness. In *The Culture and
Commerce of the American Short Story*, Andrew Levy points to
two significant periods in the development of the genre in the
twentieth century. One is "the creation and popularity of a system of how-to handbooks and courses [on short story writing]
during the period 1910-1935, concomitant with the period during which the short story had its highest value in the commercial
market" (48). Levy reproduces a document in his text that lists
the number of stories published in twenty-eight major American
mass circulation magazines from August 1927 to June 1928. The
figures are quite astonishing: 1,417 short stories appeared in the
period, 334 of them in the *Saturday Evening Post* alone.[4] During
the period 1910-35, which Levy describes as the point when the

short story had its highest commercial value, the merit of magazine short fiction was called into question by critics, because of its "uneasy intersection of the fields of literature and commerce," in which "the physical configuration of the commercial magazine, which arranged fiction and advertising on the same page, represented a perfect example of the contamination that had taken place" (50).[5] Bourdieu notes that, "The opposition between the 'commercial' and the 'non-commercial'...is the generative principle of most of the judgements which, in the theatre, cinema, painting or literature, claim to establish the frontier between what is and what is not art" (*Field* 82).

The other significant period in the popularization of the short story, according to Levy, is that of the democratization of the producer him or herself. Levy observes that, while how-to handbooks proliferated in the early half of this century, the producibility of the short story was fostered in the latter half by the "development of the system of academic workshop and graduate programs, concomitant with the near-demise of the short story as a commercial product and its rebirth as an academic genre with second-hand commercial implications" (48). Levy remarks that creative writing programs are now found in one-third of all American high schools. Moreover, each year, the 250 graduate writing programs in American universities turn out 1,500 "would-be writers of *literature*, of whom approximately half will attempt to publish short stories" (48, n65). Obviously, whether the genre is identified with how-to manuals and handbooks or with workshops and academic programs, both developments lead to the damning conclusion that *anyone* can write a short story, that it is an "apprentice" form in which one works until ready to take on the challenge of the novel or more experimental prose modes. And, of course, according to the charismatic ideology of literary creation, if anyone can do it, then it can't be art.

Yet some commentators insist that the short story genre *is* high art. For example, Nobel Prize winner William Faulkner says that the short story is "the most demanding form after poetry" and ascribes his place as a novelist to his failure to master either of the other two genres (123). In "The Short Story and the Novel,"

Alberto Moravia compares the work of Maupassant and Chekhov to that of Flaubert and Dostoyevsky and argues that the short story writers present a world that is "wider and more varied," that they give the reader "an incomparable picture of life in France and Russia of their time" (47). Beyond breadth, Moravia defends the story as less structured, and more intuitive. In essence, he says, the story is less ideologically rigid than the novel. For Moravia, ideology is the most important structural difference between the short story and the novel, "that is the skeleton of the theme from which the flesh of the story takes its form. In other words the novel has a bone structure holding it together from top to toe, whereas the short story is, so to speak, boneless" (149). Furthermore, Moravia locates ideology in the plot and characterization of the novel as well as in its structure: "The twists and turns of the plot [of the novel]...are never due to extrinsic interventions by the author or to what we could call the inexhaustible resources of life, but to the dialectical and necessary development of the ideological themes" (150). Finally, he describes the characters in the short story as "lyrical intuitions" while those in the novel are "symbols" (150).

The ideological aspect of the novel/short story debate is especially pertinent to Munro. While Moravia hints at gender in his article, using the word "intuitive" (a word usually aligned with the "feminine") to describe the short story, Desmond Pacey articulates the ideological masculinist contours of the novel form very clearly in a disparaging review of a Morley Callaghan novel which the critic regards as inferior to the author's short stories. Pacey comments: "the short story can be made out of a moment of insight, a compassionate glimpse of suffering humanity. Of the novel, however, we demand a firm philosophy, a clearly articulated sense of values" (211). I'd like to draw attention to the "feminine" language used to describe the short story: adjectives like "compassionate" and "suffering," nouns like "insight" and "humanity," suggest the intuitive, the heart, while "glimpse" and "moment" give a sense of the formal brevity of the genre. Compare this to the words Pacey uses to define the novel: the descriptors are the no-nonsense, male-associated words "firm," "clear" and "articulate," while the nouns that describe the form are "values" and "philosophy," suggesting the head, the intellectual. Even the verbs Pacey uses are instructive; that which describes the short story is passive—"can be made"—while the novel requires the active verb "demand."

In fact, the relationship between (female) gender and (short story) genre is worth exploring. Clare Hanson suggests that "the short story has been from its inception a particularly appropriate vehicle for the expression of the ex-centric, alienated vision of women" (3). Gail Scott, in "Shaping a Vehicle for Her Use," undertakes to answer the question of why women writers are attracted to short fiction. For Scott, the most obvious reasons are time and money: "First, in terms of time, a woman's life is never simple; she must put aside her writing to do a million other things. Indeed, her socialization has taught her to keep her mind so cluttered with details that it is often difficult for her to concentrate for whole days at a time in order to deal with a longer work like a novel. Then too a story is easier to sell than a longer piece" (187).

The issue of time and money is particularly difficult for young mothers (which Munro was, for the first twenty or so years of her career).[6] Tillie Olsen points out that:

> Motherhood means being instantly interruptible, responsive, responsible. Children need one *now* (and remember, in our society, the family must often try to be the center for love and health the outside world is not). The very fact that there are needs of love, not duty, that one feels them as one's self; *that there is no one else to be responsible for these needs*, gives them primacy. It is distraction, not meditation, that becomes habitual; interruption, not continuity; spasmodic, not constant, toil. (33; emphasis in original)

Distraction, interruption, spasm versus meditation, continuity, constancy. It is easy to see how the circumstances of many women's lives do not translate too well into the ideological form of the novel. Munro has said, "When I think of male writers...I can't tell you how horrified I feel when I go to a male writer's house and see *the Study*, you know, the entire house set up for

him to work." Interestingly, however, she goes on to suggest that
the male writer's position is not particularly enviable: "I just
can't help thinking *poor bugger*. What a load to carry, it's really
got to work, that novel, if everybody else is sacrificing for it"
("Writing's Something I Did" E1). Obviously Munro, as a wife and
mother, is accustomed to working around the family schedule,
not asking others to "sacrifice" for her work—which gives her
some leeway and allows for false starts and failures.

  Scott likewise posits an ideological dimension to the attraction of women writers to the short story genre, namely that its
relatively brief history makes it less rule-bound:

> The short story is one of the existing genres for which there
> are few firmly established conventions. This tends to confuse
> the little censor lurking within all of us, the little man who rep-
> resents literary norms and criteria, thus giving us space to
> play with more feminine rhythms and concepts of time and
> space....[It] gives us the latitude to avoid linear time, the
> cause-and-effect time of patriarchal logic. (187)

In the *Paris Review* interview, Munro makes a comment that certainly suggests her own awareness of that "little censor," when
she recalls the day she began to write *Lives of Girls and Women*:
"It was in January, a Sunday. I went down to the bookstore,
which wasn't open Sundays, and locked myself in. My husband
had said he would get dinner, so I had the afternoon. I remember looking around at all the great literature that was around me
and thinking, 'You fool! What are you doing here?'" (237). However, Munro says, she overcame self-censorship, went up to the
office, and began to write "Princess Ida." But then, once into the
material, Munro confesses:

> I made a big mistake. I tried to make it a regular novel, an
> ordinary sort of childhood adolescence novel. About March I
> saw it wasn't working. It didn't *feel* right to me, and I thought
> I would have to abandon it. I was very depressed. Then it
> came to me that what I had to do was pull it apart and put it
> in the story form. Then I could handle it. That's when I
> learned that I was never going to write a real novel because
> I could not think that way. (237; my emphasis)

To Munro, the "ordinary" novel doesn't "feel" right, because she can't "think that way." To "think that way" is perhaps to think in a linear fashion, to articulate a "firm philosophy," as per Desmond Pacey. The opposition of the words "think" and "feel" is important in Munro's discussions of genre. For example, in an interview with Tim Struthers in *Probable Fictions*, Munro again discusses the moment when she decided that trying to write *Lives of Girls and Women* as a traditional novel was not working: "I didn't *think* about what I was doing. I just went back and started tearing it apart and putting it into these little sections, because that's the way I wanted to tell the story to myself" ("Real" 14). Munro's desire to "tell the story to" herself in a particular way is partly a function of what Bourdieu terms the "habitus," defined as: "a "feel for the game," a "practical sense"...that inclines agents to act and react in specific situations in a manner that is not always calculated and that is not simply a question of conscious obedience to rules....The habitus is the result of a long process of inculcation, beginning in early childhood, which becomes a 'second sense' or a second nature" (Johnson 5). Certainly, in discussing her own work, and especially in pondering her difficulties in producing a novel, Munro's habitus is evident in the way she uses the words "think" and "feel," and in the metaphors she used to describe her understanding of the two different genres and her own writing process. In general, "think" is applied to what she "ought" to be doing, and "feel" pertains to what she actually does. For example, in attempting to write a novel, Munro says "I don't feel this pulling on a rope to get to the other side that I have to feel" (Struthers, "Real" 15). About composing a story, Munro opposes the images of a "road" (which is linear, like a rope) and a "house":

> So obviously I don't take up a story and follow it as if it were a road, taking me somewhere, with views and neat diversions along the way. I go into it, and move back and forth and settle here and there, and stay in it for a while. It's more like a house....I want to make a certain kind of structure and I know the feeling I want to get from being inside that structure. This is the hard part of the explanation, where I have to

use a word like "feeling," which is not very precise, because
if I attempt to be more intellectually respectable I will have to
be dishonest. "Feeling" will have to do. (Munro, "What Is
Real" 224)

For Munro, this "indescribable 'feeling'...is like the soul of the
story" (224). The ideological implications of the novel form are
apparent in these commentaries. A novel is linear, it is a road or
a rope, a form for people who think a certain way, who accept
what Scott calls "linear time, the cause-and-effect time of patriarchal logic" (187). Munro's habitus, however, leads her to a
"feeling," which is her honest view of her process, but one that
is not "intellectually respectable," not "precise." Her stories have
a "soul," and the image of their construction is, for her, the
domestic image of a house. The gender implications of the opposition of these two ways of describing the genres are obvious.

The implication of Canadian-ness is evident too, in a remark
that Munro makes about another "failed" novel, "Something I've
Been Meaning to Tell You"; the author says that this material
began as a novel, but then it "all boiled down like maple syrup"
(Twigg, "What Is" 16) to its present form—a short story. The
image is not only domestic, but also suggestively Canadian. In
interviews, Munro tends to list as her major influences writers
who are, primarily, American, female, and "Southern" (as in
"regional") practitioners of the short story such as Eudora Welty,
Katherine Anne Porter, Flannery O'Connor, and Carson
McCullers. She does this at least partially because "There was a
*feeling* that women could write about the freakish and the mar-
ginal," and that the natural genre for this freakishness and mar-
ginality is the short story, described by Munro as "our territory,
whereas the mainstream big novel about real life was men's territory" (McCulloch and Simpson 255; my emphasis).

Janice Kulyk Keefer alerts us, however, to the dangerous essentialism of suggesting that "the female mind...is more at home in
the short story, whereas the novel, with its wide range and scope,
must be a more naturally male preserve" (170). It is fascinating to
note how Keefer uses the domestic image of "home" juxtaposed
with the sense of space and movement and the outdoors in her

remarks on the novel's "wide range" and "scope." Keefer argues that it is not "habitus" or natural inclination but practical matters such as space and time that lead Canadian women writers like Munro and Gallant to the short story genre. She cites Munro's marriage and motherhood as factors, and Gallant's dependence on her writing "for her economic survival; in the days before mega-advances, short stories would have produced quicker economic results, more often" (170). Gallant was also a working journalist, and thus accustomed to writing short pieces.

While the practical is certainly a factor, and essentialism certainly risks a dangerous limitation on women's creativity, the evidence suggests that a part of women's attraction to the short story genre lies in its relative freedom from restraints of dominant ideology, as compared to the novel. Mary Eagleton, in "Gender and Genre," suggests that "Perhaps for some women writers their interest in this form has arisen, not from their belief that it is known and safe, but from their hope that the flexible, open-ended qualities of the short story may offer a transforming potential, an ability to ask the unspoken question, to raise new subject matter" (65). Eagleton thus posits a critical view of the short story that is "non-essentialist, non-reductive, yet subtly alive to the links between gender and genre" (66).

Though Canada may be considered a more welcoming market for the short story than the United States because of this country's relatively brief cultural history, its relatively small and well-educated audience, and its somewhat less entrenched literary ideology, genre privilege is still an issue. In "Calgary, Canonization, and Class," Lawrence Mathews explores the relation between issues of social class and the canon: he suggests that the novels selected as "most important" at the 1978 Calgary Conference on the Canadian Novel share not only a "conservatism of technique" but also a similarity in content:

> these novels tend to focus almost exclusively on the growth or development of an individual. The protagonist's success or failure turns on his or her ability to make correct choices according to a set of values which may vary slightly form [sic] novel to novel but is always (in the broad sense) humanist

and is always clearly spelled out for the reader. Social or
political reality, if it exists at all, is no more than a backdrop
for the protagonist's quest for self-knowledge, self-fulfillment,
or self-something else. (165)

Obviously, this ideological conservatism impinges on the accept-
ability of the short story as well; it is difficult to describe a character's lifelong quest for self-realization within the limits of the
short story.

Mathews also compares the way in which canonization occurs
in the United States and Canada. He begins by citing Richard
Ohmann's "The Shaping of a Canon: U.S. Fiction 1960-1975."
Ohmann describes a two-stage process similar to that formu-
lated by Andrew Levy. The first stage involves the world of commerce: "book buyers, agents, editors, advertisers, and reviewers,
whose work, collectively, constitutes a screening process which
resulted in the identification of a relatively small number of novels as 'compelling, important'" (qtd. in Mathews 154). Stage two
involves the separation of popular and serious literature, the latter type receiving attention from "an elite group of about eight
journals," which attracts the attention of academics, who there-
upon place the text on their course syllabuses. In this second
stage, "the college classroom and its counterpart, the academic
journal,...have become in our society the final arbiters of literary merit" (qtd. in Mathews 154).[7] However, as Mathews
observes, in Canada:

Ohmann's first stage, preliminary commercial success, need
not occur at all (As For Me and My House), or if it does, there
need not be a demonstrable connection between bestseller-
dom and canonization (The Mountain and the Valley). Nor is
the first part of Ohmann's second stage, the singling out of
the novel by an elite group of trend-setting journals, relevant.
Virtually all of the action in Canada occurs at the very end of
the process, the simultaneous embracing of a work by the
classroom and the academic journal. (155)

Kent Thompson, in "The Canadian Short Story in English and the
Little Magazines–1971," concurs in his examination of the short

fiction scene in Canada. He notes the paucity of mass circulation markets, as well as the tendency of the little magazines to be either university affiliated, government subsidized, or both, and he concludes that while the lack of "a market, a large readership, or criticism" (18) may be liberating in some ways, still "in Canadian short story publishing, there is always an impulse toward an academy technique" (18).[8]

Unfortunately for Munro, one of the strongest academic constraints in Canada, as elsewhere, is the privileging of the novel over the short story. While the story is a good teaching tool, it is the study of the novel that is traditionally used to fully challenge students as prose readers; normally the syllabus of a first-year English course in the two genres includes four or five novels, and a selection of short stories presented through an anthology. Teaching a short story collection by a single author was—until quite recently—a rare choice.

In *Taking Stock*, the proceedings of the 1978 Calgary conference on the novel, the privileging of the longer work of fiction over the shorter is evident. Short story collections are not even included on the ballot, because as Hallvard Dahlie points out in his introduction, the goal of the conference was "to articulate and celebrate the stature that the Canadian *novel* had by virtue of its own intrinsic qualities already achieved" (3; emphasis mine). However, Dahlie then goes on, throughout his discussion, to use the words "fiction" and "novel" interchangeably, as in "What the conference articulated above all was the maturity and richness of Canadian *fiction*" (3; emphasis mine).

The ballot for List A, the top one hundred, includes Munro's *Lives of Girls and Women* and Gallant's *The Pegnitz Junction*. In the voting, Munro places eighteenth, and does not make it onto List B, the top ten; Gallant does not place on either list (Steele 151-54,161-64).

Bourdieu has pointed out how difficult it is to pinpoint all the complex issues, impediments, and tensions implicit in any literary position-taking in the cultural field, but here, I think, is one very suggestive piece of evidence of the impact of genre bias on the work of an individual author. I can confirm that Munro was aware of the conference through a letter from Douglas Gibson, dated 7 February 1978, mentioning "you may see me at Calgary at this (irreverence surfaces) ridiculous conference on the novel" (MsC 38.1.75.2). The conference took place 16-18 February. My contention is that the Calgary Conference played a role in the production of Munro's fourth book, *Who Do You Think You Are?*. As part of the cultural milieu in which the work was produced, the way in which the Calgary Conference inscribed genre privilege must certainly have been a factor in what Helen Hoy calls "the complicated editorial history [of] this collection" (60). The details of this complex history are explored below, but first, the following example from Bourdieu is useful in understanding the relationship between "the unconscious strategies engendered by habitus and strategies consciously produced in response to a situation designed in accordance with the schemes of the habitus":

> The manuscripts a publisher receives are the product of a kind of pre-selection by the authors themselves according to their image of the publisher who occupies a specific position within the space of publishers. The authors' image of their publisher, which may have oriented the production, is itself a function of the objective relationship between the positions authors and publishers occupy in the field. The manuscripts are, moreover, coloured from the outset by a series of determinations...stemming from the relationship between the author's position in the field of production (unknown young author, consecrated author, house author, etc.) and the publisher's position within the system of production and circulation ("commercial" publisher, consecrated or avant-garde). They usually bear the marks of the intermediary whereby they came to the publisher...and whose authority, once again, is a function of respective positions in the field. Because subjective intentions and unconscious dispositions contribute to the efficacy of the objective structures to which they are adjusted, their interlacing tends to guide agents to their 'natural niche' in the structure of the field. (*Field* 133-34)

In early 1978, Munro finds herself occupying two very different positions in the cultural field at the same time. In Canada, she is an established author of three books, is the winner of a

Governor General's Award, and is beginning to achieve academic consecration. Robert Thacker's bibliography of works on Alice Munro notes fifty-seven entries by February 1978, ranging from biographies in companions, surveys, bibliographies, and histories of Canadian literature to scholarly articles in such journals as *World Literature Written in English, Studies in Short Fiction, Canadian Fiction Magazine,*and *Modern Fiction Studies.* Also, between 1972 and 1978, Munro's work has also been the subject of eleven theses or dissertations (including Thacker's own MA thesis). In the United States, however, Munro is a beginner, a relative unknown who has not yet found her "natural niche." She is newly published in the *New Yorker,* certainly, but she has yet to produce her first book with an American publisher. Thus, the evolution of the text known as *Who Do You Think You Are?* in Canada and as *The Beggar Maid* in the United States is much affected by the competing requirements of these two different cultural fields. In fact, the Gibson correspondence provides a telling point of contrast between the Canadian market, in which Munro has a sure foothold, and the American market, which she has entered through her association with Barber less than eighteen months before, and in which the tension between the actual and the ideological aspects of the author function are more transparent.

After publishing her first three books with McGraw-Hill Ryerson, Munro, by the mid-seventies, is considering a change to Macmillan, after being approached to that end by Douglas Gibson. The archive contains a polite letter of introduction, dated August 1974, and then, six months later, a generous and open offer:

> We understand fully that your current position [as writer in residence at Western] makes demands on your time which will not allow you to begin work on your fiction at least until the summer. This does not deter us in any way; we are confident that you will produce a book in your own good time which we shall be proud to publish. Accordingly, if you could let me know what delivery date for the manuscript you consider reasonable and what you would expect by way of an advance. (MsC 37.2.20.3)

For Munro to be invited to set her own completion date and to
state her expectations of an advance is an indication of the
power she has achieved on the Canadian scene. No doubt
because of his obvious eagerness to sign Munro, Gibson is also
equable on the question of genre, though his letter of 23
December 1975 indicates an awareness of Munro's genre-anxiety
in the following remark: "In the meantime please keep me
posted on your feelings about the next batch (it's a lovely
expression and has no hint of disrespect) of short stories. We'd
be very pleased to draw up a contract at any time that the idea
appeals to you" (MsC 37.2.20.5). Gibson is polite, but determined; in February 1976, he reminds Munro, "Anytime that you
are far enough advanced with the writing to become formally
involved with us, we, like Barkis, 'is willin'"" (MsC 37.2.20.6). By
7 February 1978 Gibson is close to making a deal with Munro,
but he must clear a couple of hurdles first. It is possible that she
has asked for more money. Because financial information is
restricted, I can't be sure of that, though according to Geoff
Hancock, the paperback rights for Munro's second Macmillan
book, *The Moons of Jupiter*, were sold for $45,000, the highest
price for a work of Canadian fiction ever recorded (187). The
Gibson correspondence for this period also mentions the forthcoming publication by Macmillan of a novel by Munro's father,
Robert Laidlaw, titled *The McGregors* (MsC 38.1.75.2), as well as
a job interview Gibson conducted with Munro's daughter (MsC
38.13.14). I mention these two items only to support my suggestion that, in Canada, Munro is negotiating with her new publisher from a position of relative power and authority—well-
earned power resulting from her publishing history and the
recognition her work has received. The above-mentioned letter
turns out to be the penultimate letter before his contract with
Munro is signed; after mentioned *The MacGregors* and the job
interview, Gibson returns to his familiar refrain: "I wonder if you
are now close to having a book-length collection and therefore
to drawing up a contract with us. I can think of no author I
would rather have on Macmillan's list." Gibson's tenacity eventually pays off: A letter dated 28 April 1978, begins "Welcome to

Macmillan" and invites Munro to leave the contractual details to publisher and agent, while he and Munro prepare the forthcoming book for a fall publication.

The book contracted to Macmillan is a short story collection. Gibson proposes the title "True Lies: Stories by Alice Munro," taken from a line in the story "Providence." From his discussion of the ordering of the stories, it's possible to guess that the collection comprises several "Rose" stories, some "Simon" stories, and other unrelated stories, including "Accident," "Chaddeleys and Flemings," and "Characters." Gibson proposes putting the Rose stories at the end, in order to avoid confusing the reader; yet on the other hand, he does not want Munro to "anonymize" some of the Rose stories, which Munro must have been trying to do to make the book more of a collection and less of a story sequence. On this point, Gibson says: "The heroine of 'The Beggar Maid,' for example, is clearly Rose; I suggest that you should think twice before plucking too many Roses" (MsC 37.2.20.7b). What Gibson's letter makes clear is that the planned book is neither a novel nor a short story sequence, though several stories appear to be "linked" by focusing on the same character, either Rose or Simon. While Munro's habitus of the (sometimes linked) short story is acceptable to her Canadian publisher, the picture on the other side of the border is somewhat different, and the pressure from her American connections to produce a novel mounts as the year progresses.

As Frank Davey has commented, literary publishing in English Canada in the 1970s remained in the "petty-commodity" mode ("Writers" 95), in which publishers do not unduly influence the form and content of the text, or pay too much attention to its marketability. In the United States, however, the publishing game is not nearly so laissez-faire. In fact, Munro begins a working relationship with Norton editor Sherry Huber some time before signing a contract with the company. From 1976 to 1978, Barber has been busily circulating Munro's stories. When "The Beggar Maid" appears in the *New Yorker* in June 1977, it generates a great deal of interest. Though a formal contract between Munro and Norton is not signed until 19 May 1978, it is clear from correspondence in the archive that a dialogue between Huber and Munro about the shape of that book is already well underway. While Macmillan was happy to publish a collection of unrelated or partially linked short stories, Munro's American publisher was rather insistent that the stories be linked closely.

In "Rose and Janet: Alice Munro's Metafiction," Helen Hoy has produced a lengthy and meticulous study of the "tortuous" (69) publication history of Munro's fourth book. Hoy explains:

> Before Alice Munro's *Who Do You Think You Are?* appeared in the fall of 1978, her anticipated new collection of stories was announced as *Rose and Janet*. The first reviews, although about a book entitled *Who Do You Think You Are?*, described a collection unlike the one soon available in bookstores, the one we know. In *Books in Canada*, for example, Wayne Grady discussed the mirror stories of twin heroines, "Rose, who grows up in West Hanratty, Ont., the child of a defeated father and a powerless but compassionate stepmother named Flo; and Janet, who is from Dagleish [*sic*], the child of an equally ineffectual father and a somewhat non-existent mother." (59)

The title *Who Do You Think You Are?* takes on quite a different resonance when the book is described this way. In fact, Janet is a writer, and the closing stories suggest that she has been the "creator" of Rose, the actress. Why did this book not appear? In Hoy's account:

> Doug Gibson, Munro's editor, explained Munro's sudden decision to revise the book when she realized that Rose and Janet were the same person, a decision which meant literally stopping the presses one Monday morning in mid-September while Munro, who stayed in Toronto overnight, revised, copy-editors proof-read, the press rewrote the flap copy, and the printers ordered more paper. *Who Do You Think You Are?*, as we know it, with ten third-person stories about Rose, was off to press two days later, in time for its November 18 publication deadline. The decision cost Munro $1,864. (59)

Hoy identifies no less than seven different proposed forms of the book, the most significant of which are outlined in Table 1. She comments that "The tension between a Rose version of the material and a 'Rose and other stories' arrangement, which almost culminated in two independent Norton and Macmillan publications, manifested itself time and again during the editing process" (60-1). But like Doug Gibson's explanation that Munro simply "realized that Rose and Janet were the same person," Hoy's analysis ultimately boils down to the mystery of the creative process: she says that in achieving the final version, "Munro had finally created the arrangement she felt to be artistically right" (69). Hoy acknowledges that "fortuitous factors extraneous to the individual stories...[such as] the inclinations of editors—may influence the direction of artistic revision and experimentation" (70), but given the evidence which she mentions, and which I discuss in detail, she severely understates the case.

The archive contains four letters from Munro to Sherry Huber at Norton. The first is undated; it is a brief note scribbled in Munro's hand on the torn-off front cover of a drugstore writing pad. It appears to have been sent to Huber in a box along with some revised manuscripts. I can safely assume a mid-May 1978 date for this document, because Munro refers to the recently sent box in her next two letters, both dated 19 May. I can also confirm that Huber received this first, undated, scribbled-on-cardboard letter, because several comments that appear to be Huber's are written there. All three letters propose somewhat different configurations for the book.[9]

Huber's notes on the undated letter suggest that Munro's attempts to make Rose the central character of all the stories have not worked (MsC 38.2.64.3). Obviously, Munro has been asked by Norton to make all the stories about Rose, but she is having difficulty doing so. In her marginalia, Huber plans her strategy: "be strong, sound positive with Alice. Call Ginger before final conference" (MsC 38.2.64.3). Apparently, Huber recognizes that Munro must be treated with firm resolve in this matter, must be encouraged to believe that she can "novelize"

Table 1
Evolution of *Who Do You Think You Are?*

| 1. Configuration of Macmillan version, May 1978 [a] | 2. Structure of Macmillan Rose and Janet manuscript, August 1978 [b] | 3. Norton's "deservedly abandoned" novel, September 1978 [c] | 4. *Who Do You Think You Are?* fall 1978 [d] |
|---|---|---|---|
| Title: *Rose and Janet* | Rose: | Royal Beatings | Royal Beatings |
| | Royal Beatings | Privilege | Privilege |
| A Rose section: | Privilege | Half a Grapefruit | Half a Grapefruit |
| Royal Beatings | Half a Grapefruit | Characters | Wild Swans |
| Privilege | Wild Swans | Nerve (Wild Swans) | The Beggar Maid |
| Half a Grapefruit | The Beggar Maid | The Beggar Maid | Mischief |
| Wild Swans | Spelling | Mischief | Providence |
| Spelling | | Providence | Simon's Luck |
| The Beggar Maid | Janet: | Simon's Luck | Spelling |
| Accident | | Spelling | Who Do You Think |
| | Connection | | You Are? |
| Followed by a Janet section: | The Stone in the Field | | |
| Chaddeleys and Flemings | Mischief | | |
| Mischief | Providence | | |
| Providence | The Moons of Jupiter | | |
| Moons of Jupiter | Who Do You Think You Are? | | |
| and a new story Munro is | | | |
| working on called | | | |
| Who Do You Think You Are? | | | |

a  Described in Munro's letter to Sherry Huber, 19 May (MsC 38.2.64.4).
b  See Hoy. Simon's Luck was to be added as a Rose story after rewrite.
c  Described in Sherry Huber's last letter, 12 September 1978 (MsC 38.2.64.10).
d  Published by Macmillan Canada, fall 1978. *The Beggar Maid*, published in the United State by Alfred A. Knopf in April 1979 and in Britain by Allan Lane in 1980 contains the same stories in the same order. The only difference is the title.

these stories. It is also clear that Barber is part of this negotiation, though, oddly, the six-month gap in the correspondence noted in the previous chapter occurs during this period.[10] To unearth this correspondence would be very useful, because when Barber writes to Munro four times in June 1978, the idea of a "novel-like" structure for the book is very much on her mind. For example, in a letter of 20 June, Barber sends Munro a copy of *Earthly Possessions,* and comments on how Anne Tyler created a novel out of a series of stories about a single character (MsC 38.2.63.12).

In the first of the dated letters to Huber, Munro asserts that while "Royal Beatings," "Privilege," "Half a Grapefruit," "Characters," "Wild Swans," "Spelling," and "Beggar Maid" are stories about Rose, others—the central characters of "Mischief" and "Providence"—are not. The irony that these two stories are now very much about Rose in the "definitive" text is inescapable. However, it is also interesting to note that other stories proposed for this collection but later published in *The Moons of Jupiter* began as "Janet" stories and have remained so, namely "Chaddeleys and Flemings," and "The Moons of Jupiter," which feature a central character named Janet, who is a writer, divorced from Richard, and mother of Nichola and Judith.

The solution that Munro proposes is a split between Rose stories and Janet stories (see Table 1, column 1) in two almost equal parts. Munro tells Huber that Macmillan is doing this with the Canadian version, but with the story "Accident" in the middle, and "Chaddeleys and Flemings" divided into two stories. (MsC 38.2.64.4a-d).

Munro's second letter, of the same date, proposes a similar configuration, with the addition of "Characters" (an uncollected story) to the Rose section. Munro adds that she has mailed a rewrite of "Simon's Luck," which has somehow changed, in her thinking, from a "Janet" story to a "Rose" story (MsC 38.2.64.5a).

These two letters raise several questions. How does one story become a "Rose" story and another a "Janet" story? Did Munro suddenly "realize" that Janet and Rose were "the same person"? If so, what external pressures and internalized beliefs combined to create this realization? Point of view is an interesting aspect; the archive reveals how Munro attempted to write the Rose and Janet stories in every possible configuration of narrative viewpoint—first/third, third/first, all first, all third. It's an amusing sidenote that the Norton version had been planned as first person, but the definitive text is in the third person because in September 1978, that's how Macmillan had already printed the first few stories of Rose and Janet, and to reprint those early stories in first person was simply too costly (Hoy 69).

Another question is which of these letters were ever sent. The Munro archive contains *no* outgoing correspondence at all, with the exception of these four letters. Obviously, the undated note must have been sent and received, because Huber's handwriting is visible on the document. If so, was it sent back to Munro with the box of manuscripts? Otherwise, how could it be in the collection? Similarly, what about the other two long letters both dated 19 May? Were they ever sent, or are they present in the archive because another letter, describing a completely different book, was the one actually sent to Sherry Huber at Norton?

In Helen Hoy's examination of the editorial dialogue between Huber and Munro, she notes Huber's input on the ordering of the stories. Hoy asserts that the Norton version was to be *all* Rose, Huber having presumably rejected the Rose and Janet idea of the Macmillan version. Furthermore, Huber changed the title "Wild Swans" to "Nerve" because "she liked the *progression* from privilege to nerve to providence and luck in Rose's perception of life" (Hoy 68; my emphasis). Hoy notes Huber's preference for narrative linearity as well: "Uncomfortable with narrative gaps and discontinuities, Huber also suggested conventional transitions" (68). Finally, says Hoy, Huber also explicitly indicated a preference for the first person. All of these preferences point to the ideology of the conventional novel—continuity, first person, progression, linearity, connection—indicating the ideological struggle that underlies the supposedly "artistic" negotiation between author and editor. Hoy concludes, "Norton's never-published novel *The Beggar Maid*—its conventional structure deservedly abandoned—was the catalyst for Munro's sudden decision to stop the presses at Macmillan" (68) (see Table 1, Column 3). I question the logic of this statement, because the version now deemed authoritative and definitive, and published by Macmillan in Canada in 1978 and Knopf in the United States in 1979, is far more like this "deservedly abandoned" "novel" than any of the previous configurations, though unlike the Norton version in that the text is written in third-person-focused point of view, and does not give conventional narrative transitions, so that each story is capable of standing on its own. Hoy cites a letter from Munro to Huber dated 19 September 1978,[11] in which the author says, "After you said you liked [the rewrite of] Simon's Luck, I got more and more convinced that the series of Rose stories was the only way to do this book and that the Macmillan book was a dreadful awkward waste of good material" (68-69). Munro apparently wrote these words to her American editor from the Macmillan offices where her last-minute transformation of the text was underway. After examining the archival evidence, I must disagree with Hoy's assertion that, in the published version, "Munro had finally created the arrangement she felt to be artistically right" (69). To me, the evidence points to a bewildering assortment of external pressures—the Calgary Conference and the equability of the Canadian market compared to the novelizing pressures from Huber and Barber—combined with internal forces such as Munro's own strong drive to achieve American publication, to work in the genre in which she "feels" at home, and to maintain her own position in the "hierarchically structured space" (Bourdieu, *Field* 95) of the cultural field. For one thing, what is the significance of the statement that Huber's liking for "Simon's Luck" suddenly made the Rose sequence fall into place?

The 19 September letter noted above is Munro's last communication with Sherry Huber, who left the employ of W.W. Norton early in the fall of 1978. Munro's contractual agreement to publish with Norton collapsed at around the same time, though the relationship between Huber's departure and the demise of the Norton deal is unclear. Munro's contract was then picked up by Knopf; Barber encloses the Norton release form and the Knopf contract in the same letter, dated 7 November 1978 (MsC 38.2.63.16), and the letter from Knopf editor Ann Close welcoming Munro to the company is dated 13 November (MsC 38.1.3.5). Barber's covering letter of 7 November mentions that Huber is looking for work and might need Munro to provide a reference. It's not unreasonable to speculate that for several weeks that fall, Munro was without an American publisher, a fact which may well have stimulated her to find the form of a story sequence "artistically right." Even more ironic is the fact that, after all of Huber's efforts, the Knopf editors chose the Canadian version of the book over Norton's (38.1.3.5). All they wanted to change was the title.

*Who Do You Think You Are?* is the last "linked" work Munro has produced. I would argue that this text is Munro's final and glorious bow to the privileging of the novel over the short story. Once she has fully entered into her habitus and located her art in the short story form, without defensiveness or apology (except occasionally on *Morningside*), she, like Flaubert in his own time, has transformed the field.

Hoy appears to put her faith in the concept of the authoritative text. She describes "the author's subjective experience of an abrupt and thoroughgoing flash of insight, the bathwater-displacing Eureka moment of revelation" (70) as the moment when Munro decides to make the text Rose-only, at her own expense. What such an analysis fails to take into account is that Munro was shut out of the Calgary Conference by virtue of genre; that Sherry Huber's departure from Norton seems to have left Munro temporarily without an American publisher; and that the Macmillan book had a looming deadline. As Munro points out to Tim Struthers: "A book cannot go on the Canadian market later than about mid-November, or its chances for Christmas sales are just dead. So we had to get it out by that time. All of which things, having been a bookseller, I understand" ("Real" 31). Bourdieu asserts that "to utter 'in public' the true nature of the field, and of its mechanisms, is sacrilege *par excellence*, the unforgivable sin which all the censorships in the field seek to repress" (*Field* 73). Munro appears to realize that in the previous comment she has sinned against the field, because she then adds, haltingly,

> You see it was mostly a....It wasn't an artistic decision as much....Well, it was. In the end it was *my* decision for what the book had to be. But the decisions before that were made from a publishing point of view, with me going along with them because I couldn't, at that time, see how I could alter things. I couldn't see if I would ever get enough stories to make a Rose book. In this I was helped by the patience of my American publisher who seemed, with good reason, less commercially nervous than a Canadian publisher, and who was willing to wait to see what I could do. ("Real" 31-32)

Though both the Macmillan and Norton contracts were signed on 20 June 1978 (Hoy 67), the publication deadline for Macmillan was 18 November of that year, while the Americans required a completed draft by late September 1978 for a spring 1979 publication (MsC 38.2.64.9). The question, therefore, is whether the Americans are more patient or simply required a longer lead time for production and promotion in their far larger literary market. It is also possible that the longer production schedule reflected the American publisher's uncertainty about an unknown Canadian writer.

For Hoy, the received version is a "hurdle" that we see Munro "attempt...several times, each time acquiring new resources" (70) until she reaches "the conviction, sense of inevitability, and facility of the final creative leap" (70). Given the archival evidence I have presented, I would argue that the authoritative text is in itself a fiction, as are final creative leaps, at least leaps dissociated from cultural pressures to make money, crack the American market, write novels, think like a man, focus on the growth of the individual while subtly denouncing bourgeois values yet supporting the dominant ideology of secular humanism—all the while pretending to care only about "Art" and not at all about money.

Given the struggles Munro underwent to produce this text, the irony must have been delicious: in this year of canon-formation at Calgary, from which she was excluded by genre, the Governor General's Award for the best work of fiction in English was given to a short story sequence called *Who Do You Think You Are?* It might well have been a further and equally delicious irony for

Munro that the American version of the text, *The Beggar Maid*, earned her a nomination for the Booker Prize the following year. Bourdieu defines successful cultural producers as those "who can *recognize* the specific demands of this universe [i.e., the cultural field] and who, by concealing from themselves and others the interest at stake in their practice, obtain the means of deriving profits from disinterestedness" (*Field* 75). Obviously, the production of *Who Do You Think You Are?* forced Munro to develop her recognition of the specific demands of the literary field. What is most intriguing and inspiring about the whole episode is that, following this highly successful story sequence, instead of slavishly attempting to repeat the success of *Who Do You Think You Are?*, Munro has never returned to the story sequence form.[12]

In closing his discussion of Flaubert, Bourdieu warns his reader that the now "familiar world" of Flaubert's work and influence "keeps us from understanding, among other things, the extraordinary effort that he had to make, the exceptional resistances that he had to surmount, beginning within himself, in order to produce and impose that which, largely because of him, we now take for granted" (205-206). Munro's effort in the creation of *Who Do You Think You Are?* is reflected in her defensive reaction to Gzowski's comment on how each of the stories in *Open Secrets* is a novel; the exceptional resistance she mounted in its creation is evident in the archive; and the way in which "we now take for granted" the results of Munro's struggles is obvious in the critical appraisal of her work: Gzowski cites a review of *Open Secrets* which lavishes praise on "the incomparable Alice Munro, who is not just a good writer but a great one, the first Canada has produced" (Oct. 94). However, it is not *only* Canada which "has produced" Alice Munro; in fact, I have shown that the author function, the "plurality of selves" known as Alice Munro, has been "produced":

— by Canada *and* the United States and their respective cultural fields;

— by Robert Weaver, Virginia Barber, Charles McGrath, Sherry Huber, and Ann Close, and all those "cultural bankers in whom art and business meet in practice" (Bourdieu, *Field* 75);

— by a patriarchy that subordinates women in language and thus produces particularly potent forms of resistance;
— by such canonizers as the academy and the Calgary conference;
— by the exigencies of the marketplace and the disavowal of the economic necessary to the "accumulation of symbolic capital" (Bourdieu 75); and
— finally, in response to and engagement with all these producers, by the active but not sovereign protagonist in the struggle, the author herself, who "reinvents" the short story form in her struggle to "remake" the individual short stories in *Who Do You Think You Are?*

CHAPTER V

## "WRITER"
# Implications of Authority

Oct. 28, 1982


Dear Alice:

...I saw the nice things about you in Best American Stories—and much approved. How do you like being a one-woman renaissance?

Love, John

(MsC. 24.8.9.3)

---

Notes for chapter 5 are on p. 175

How does Munro feel about such accolades? Her correspondence with John Metcalf indicates that the public role of author makes her a little uncomfortable and more than slightly cynical.[1] The writer's life has its disadvantages: there are myriad invitations to official literary functions; there are the self-seeking and often arrogant demands of editors and publishers; there are nasty reviews and commentaries.

Munro's resistance to invitations to cultural benefits and public appearances in part stems from her understanding that such events construct *the artist as product*. Her discomfort with, for example, a rent-an-author benefit dinner (MsC. 24.8.9.6) speaks to the notion of the author as name brand, a person whose presence can be purchased to provide an evening's entertainment for a patron of the arts and his cronies. In successfully producing cultural work, the author's person, her physical presence, acquires value; she becomes a *product* herself, with a price tag attached, a construction of the author so naturalized in consumer culture that Munro might wonder whether she's alone in finding such an invitation contemptible.

Furthermore, the demands of editors, anthologists, and publishers show the author as *producer*, functioning in a real market economy that makes intrusive and sometimes unreasonable demands, as in the case of the wrangling over the form of *Who Do You Think You Are?*, discussed in chapter 4. When Munro describes her amusement at a request for a particular type of story from an American anthology editor, Metcalf responds, "a 'negatively erotic' story sounds to me pretty difficult—if not downright impossible. Possibly women in New York know something I don't" (MsC. 24.8.9.7).

Stories like "Material" reveal the problem of the artist as *citizen*. Authors live in a real world—they have families, neighbours, communities. As such, they are citizens with social lives outside their authorship, and social responsibilities to the communites in which they live—a situation that can be complicated for a writer who, like Munro, uses autobiographical and regional material in her work. In December 1981, a rather painful incident occurred when an editorial appeared in the *Wingham*

*Advance-Times* in reaction to Munro's comments in an interview about the "community of outcasts" (Twigg "What Is" 18) in which she grew up. The editorial said: "Sadly enough Wingham people have never had much chance to enjoy the excellence of [Munro's] writing ability because we have repeatedly been made the butt of soured and cruel introspection on the part of a gifted writer....It seems that something less than greatness impels her to return again and again to a time and place in her life where bitterness warped her personality" (qtd. in Wayne 9). In effect, the author of the editorial sees Munro's work as a manifestation of her personality and as an attack on the community itself.

The process by which current notions of the author as product, producer, and citizen came to be naturalized in this culture is worth examining. In his historical overview of theories of authorship, Sean Burke remarks that "Hellenic culture saw the origins of poetry in the Muse, to whom the poet was merely messenger, avatar or mouthpiece...a view [that]...at once elevates the poet or author as elect figure—set apart from the rest of humanity by a gift of divine afflatus—but deprives the author of the role of originating force" ("Changing" 5). Burke suggests that in the rethinking of the nature of authorship in the nineteenth and twentieth centuries, "this notion of alterity or 'otherness' has persisted but in a manner often transplanted from its sacred or ideal sources....Twentieth century theory has relocated the source of otherness in the unconscious or language itself" (5). But Burke remains suspicious of many contemporary constructions of authorship, such as Eliot's "classic statement of modernist impersonality" with its "ostensibly anti-romantic arguments" ("Twentieth" 65) in which poetry becomes "the emptying-out of personal feeling rather than its expression" (66). The modernist argument against the discourse of literature "as a revelation of personality" ("Reconstructing" xxiii) produced "the image of the modernist writer as disinterested artificer" and New Criticism developed the impersonalist mode, displacing "the autonomy of the subject onto the text itself" (xxiii). Barthes's work on authorship is seen by Burke as "the latest instance of the impersonalizing tendency in modernity, whereby 'writing'...now becomes the privileged category which serves to distance the text from its authorial subject" (xxiv). However, for Burke, the difficulty is that Barthes's "requisite impersonality" still associates the author with "the high romantic conception of disinterested subjectivity" (xxiv).

Burke's use of the term "romantic," as in "the romantic notion of a writer's creative genius" ("Ideologies" 216), and his definition of "modernist," as in "an artisanal view of authorship as analogous to any act of socio-economic production" (216) or as a "disinterested artificer" ("Reconstructing" xxiii), are important touchstones in my discussion of the author as *product, producer* and *citizen*. My aim is to describe the weaknesses (and similarities) of both the romantic and modernist views and to reconstruct the author as a "cultural worker," as in Weedon's "active but not sovereign protagonist" in an ideological struggle (41). The difficulty with either the romantic or modernist position is that it is, to use Thomas Docherty's term, "idealist," in the sense that "authority is located in a single proper name, distinguished from all other interfering historical factors" (55). However, for Docherty, authority,

> like speech, never happens in a void. It is always inherently "tactful," "tactical": dialogical. It is thoroughly determined by a socio-historical situation which far exceeds the capacity of any individual consciousness (writer's or reader's; lawgiver's or law-obeyer's) for intentionality or substance. ...Authority is not a matter of individual intention but is rather the effect of the interplay of various intentionalities. (56)

On the question of genre, for example, Munro's "tactful" manoeuvrings result not merely from her generic choices, but from a "tactical" interplay of intentionalities—of academics and critics intent on identifying a canon, editors intent on keeping their jobs, and publishers intent on capturing the Christmas market, to name a few.

Docherty comments in particular on Bourdieu's view that "the definition of art...is an object of struggle among the classes" (qtd. in Docherty 58). Class issues predominate in the works of

Alice Munro, yet the paradox of the field of restricted production is evident also. Munro describes herself as "lower caste," yet
claims authority. If artists are somehow above their bourgeois
audience, then, as Docherty points out, the author is in a bind:
"To be an author, one must distinguish oneself from those who
merely obey some already existing authority: one must be 'non-
conformist'…[yet] this formulation of authority, vested in the
names of certain authors, depends most immediately upon
the class affiliations of those involved in acts of canon-formation" (59). The invitation to something like a rent-an-author dinner in support of a writer's association highlights Munro's
enmeshment in a system of uncomfortable class relations, the
most obvious being that those who support the cause can afford
to spend big bucks on a charity dinner—something few working
writers could afford to do themselves.

   Munro's habitus directs her to a specific position-taking in
the cultural field: that of a serious literary author. According to
Bourdieu, for an author to achieve the desired position in the
field, "a sort of sense of social direction…is indispensable in
order to be able to navigate in a hierarchically structured space
in which movement is always fraught with the danger of losing
class" (*Field* 95). This sense of social direction leads Munro to
seek publication in prestigious journals such as the *New
Yorker*, to eschew publicity, and to construct a reticence about
the cult of the public writer—the writer as product. Bourdieu
explains that:

> This practical mastery [i.e., the habitus] gives its possessors
> a "nose" and a "feeling," *without any need for cynical calcu-
> lation*, for "what needs to be done," where to do it, how and
> with whom, in view of all that has been done and is being
> done, all those who are doing it, and where. Choosing the
> right place of publication, the right publisher, journal, gallery
> or magazine is vitally important because for each author,
> each form of production and product, there is a correspon-
> ding *natural site* in the field of production, and producers or
> products that are not in their right place are more or less
> bound to fail. (95)

Bourdieu's emphasis on the absence of "cynical calculation" is important to my argument, for though it may appear at times that this chapter critiques Munro's acts as calculated, in fact what it does is to show how her "sense of social direction," her "nose" for where she needs to be in the cultural field, is the function both of the "bad faith" of the field and of her "tactical" acquiescence and "tactful" resistance in various ideological struggles that confront her in the pursuit of literary authority. The role of the "smiling public [wo]man" wistfully described by Yeats is one that Munro resists, but complete refusal is not always possible— for example, in the necessity of promotion for her own books.

If Munro resists the notion of author as *product,* as a *producer* she shows significant "practical mastery" of the requirements of the field. For example, early in her career, Munro successfuly transformed a magazine (i.e., "popular") story called "Goodbye Myra" into a modernist literary story called "Day of the Butterfly." The qualitative gap is articulated by Robert Weaver when he returns the earlier version of the piece to Munro in January 1956, saying that it is "a pleasant story but not really as interesting as much of your other work....I think it is quite possible you may be able to interest a magazine in this story."[2] It is clear in Weaver's remarks that two different types of markets exist, and that a popular (women's?) magazine is the most suitable venue for a "pleasant" but less "interesting" piece.

"Goodbye Myra" is narrated by a child named Helen, who is recalling the persecution of a classmate named Myra. The story first appeared in *Chatelaine,* a Canadian women's magazine, in July 1956. Munro's is one of two stories that appear in that issue. The other is by Margaret Craven, titled "No Man's Good Enough for Janie." Both stories are printed with a "teaser." The teaser for the Craven story reads: "She was the Canadian working girl, grade A—well paid, well dressed, a little spoiled" (14), while Munro's reads: "I guess everyone remembers a girl like Myra at school—the different one, the outsider. I truly wanted to help her, but I was too young and afraid. Then it was too late" (17). A direct quotation from Munro's story is also prominently displayed: "Myra handed me the leatherette case. 'When I get

back—' she began, and looked at me. Suddenly I was afraid" (17).
"Goodbye Myra" is also accompanied by an illustration, credited
to an artist named William Winter. Lurid black ink on a yellow
background depicts Myra in her hospital bed, side view. She has
long dark braids, appears to be wearing full makeup, and is def-
initely non-Caucasian in appearance, probably South Asian. She
occupies the left-hand side of the illustration; on the right, and
in closeup, is a figure—the narrator—who resembles a Barbie
doll, with blonde curls, impossibly thick dark lashes, rosebud
mouth, gloves, coat, and hat. The narrator wears a perturbed
expression, while Myra has a knowing, patient look.

This same story, rewritten for a different audience, appears in
Munro's award-winning first collection, *Dance of the Happy
Shades*, under the title "Day of the Butterfly." Obviously, in this
incarnation, the story is unaccompanied by teasers, quotations,
or illustrations. The two stories end differently. The *Chatelaine*
version ends with an overt statement of the narrator's treacherous relief at being able to leave the bedside of the dying Myra.
The anthology version is more self-conscious in several ways:
while the early version ends with the narrator's emphatic
"Goodbye!" the later one returns to the larger picture of the narrator's guilt, and the "legendary uses" to which Myra and her sad
story will be put. In effect, Munro's rewrite expands a small personal incident into a commentary on life and art. The narrator
of "Goodbye Myra" is "afraid" and helpless, as the *Chatelaine*
presentation emphasizes; the narrator of "Day of the Butterfly"
is more cynical, the retrospective point of view more adult.
Munro's revisions also make the story more artful. Robert
Thacker points out that "Helen's attempt to withdraw quickly
from the room, while explicitly stated in the first version, is
more subtle in the second" ("Clear" 47); similarly, though Helen
tries to give a present back to Myra in the first version, in the
second she makes a show of accepting the "guilt-tinged offering," concluding that since she has no way to refuse the gift, she
will psychologically discard it by taking it home and allowing her
brother to "pull it apart" (110), thus implying the familiar
Canadian mode of submerged, polite racism.

Munro's holograph revisions of "Goodbye Myra" are legible on the archival copy of the story, torn from the pages of the magazine. As early as 1956, Munro had a "nose" for where she wanted to be on literary scene, a sense of what the "natural site" for her work must be. In rewriting the story for inclusion in a literary collection, Munro makes the message less explicit, more implicit. As Bader remarks in "The Structure of the Modern Short Story" (1945), "To suggest, to hint, to imply, but not to state directly or openly...is a favorite contemporary technique" (110). In *New Worlds*, a 1980 anthology of Canadian short stories aimed at the high school classroom, editor John Metcalf takes Bader's aesthetic of implication even further: "Good writers aren't usually concerned with expressing 'messages' or with *expressing their feelings*. They're concerned with *causing other people to feel and see*. They're concerned, often quite coldly, with *manipulating* your feelings" (163). In this statement, the central tenets of modernism are obvious, particularly in its reluctance to situate the writing subject sociohistorically and also in its retention of the godlike figure of the author. Modernism insists on our attention to the text, not to the author or the author's biography; in short, it invites readers to place themselves passively in a transcendent, disinterested author's hands to be manipulated, made to feel certain things.

Modernism thus disregards the subject who is speaking as author, but when the author is seen as a subject in sociohistorical discourse, as this study attempts to do, then *who* is speaking matters very much indeed.[3] Burke argues that "the notion of the author has been falsely analogised with the transcendent/impersonal subject" and that in order to "deconstruct" this view, we need to "reposition authorship as a situated activity present not so much to itself as to culture, ideology, language, difference, influence, biography" ("Reconstructing" xxvi). In short, when the author is seen neither as a superior creator nor as a neutral crafter, but rather as a cultural worker engaged in a political struggle in its most "euphemized" form, to use Bourdieu's phrase, then the question becomes, "whose interests are served by this particular ideological position?" The importance of asking this question becomes clear when I search the electronic catalogue at the Mackimmie Library and find that a film adaptation of the Munro story "Boys and Girls" is held at the Educational Media Library. It appears that Munro's literary status qualifies her to teach schoolchildren about gender roles. As Lennard Davis has pointed out, "The social reality of publication automatically conveys with it the expectation that a novelist is and must be a kind of authority on all subjects" (142). When the romantic and modernist notions of authorship are discarded in favour of the view of the author as cultural worker, then the necessity of asking questions about and analyzing the ideologies of the cultural field becomes evident indeed.

If Munro is seen as a cultural worker, the reasons why the construction of author as product, producer, and citizen chafe for her can be readily understood. An examination of the fair use statutes indicates that the writer is in a proprietary relationship with language; however, this proprietary relationship is problematized in Munro's case. As a Canadian raised in a culture that was, in her early years, still defined by its relationship to Britain, she is a "colonized subject," and as Ashcroft, Griffiths, and Tiffin point out in *The Empire Writes Back*, "One of the main features of imperial oppression is control over language.... Language becomes the medium through which a hierarchical structure of power is perpetuated, and the medium through which conceptions of 'truth,' 'order' and 'reality' become established" (7). As discussed in earlier chapters, the workings of American cultural hegemony play a key role in the publication history of *Who Do You Think You Are?* A further instance occurs on the occasion of Munro's first *New Yorker* publication, in which she is advised by Charles McGrath to indicate clearly that the story takes place in Canada, because Americans think everything takes place in the United States unless you tell them otherwise (MsC 37.2.30.2). Like many post-colonial writers, Munro subverts imperial linguistic authority in a variety of subtle ways—with her digressive narratives, her choice of the "fragmentary" genre of the short story, and especially in her open-ended and paradoxical use of language.[4]

The situation is similar in terms of gender, and the authors of *The Empire Writes Back* acknowledge that women "share with colonized races and peoples an intimate experience of the politics of oppression and repression, and like them they have been forced to articulate their experiences in the language of their oppressors" (174-75). In *The Madwoman in the Attic,* Gilbert and Gubar likewise remark on "the coercive power not only of cultural constraints but of the literary texts which incarnate them" (11). The way in which even the sisterhood of Munro and Barber is often overwhelmed by the patriarchal literary culture in which they operate is evident in their correspondence.

As discussed in chapter 4, genre comes strongly into play, the short story being identified in many quarters as a "women's" genre, and placed on the sidelines in a literary culture that privileges the novel—for its philosophy, linearity, large scope—over the short story. Thus, the genre issue has links to gender and nationality or colonial status; but genre is also tied, in some rather complex ways, to the modernist requirement of "fictiveness" or "invention," and to the aesthetics of autobiography and metafiction. If the short story ranks below the novel in the hierarchy of genres, the categories of autobiography or memoir fall even lower on the scale.

Elizabeth Meese identifies three assumptions that underlie hierarchies in literature:

> First, literary reputation is apparently reserved, particularly, for authors of imaginative works. Second, achievement in the novel, poetry, and drama—the "major" genres—is thought of greater merit than achievement in short stories, letters, diaries, children's works, travel literature and other nonfictional prose—the "minor" genres. Finally, the works are characterized as universal rather than regional. (38)

It is obvious that Munro is up against all three of these requirements in achieving the author function. I have touched on regionalism in chapter 2, and on the concept of the short story as a "minor" genre in chapter 4, but here I wish to conflate what Meese's first and second points suggest about the requirement of fictiveness. In terms of authorial imagination, Margaret Atwood has said:

> I think people do assume that women write entirely out of their own experience and that everything you read in a book by a woman is strictly autobiographical....For me that's saying women aren't capable of all those things that men are supposed to be capable of, such as craft, technique, invention, imagination and so forth. They're only supposed to be capable of writing a kind of fictionalized diary. ("Sexual Bias" 152)

When asked by Tim Struthers about the allusiveness of a passage in *Lives of Girls and Women*, Munro remarks, "I had no writer or passage in mind. I made that up. I make a lot of things up, though nobody seems to think so" ("Real" 36). On the other hand, Munro's early work, in particular, does draw heavily on her own life experience. In her later work, she turns outside her own life; she says "I'm doing less personal writing now than I used to for a very simple obvious reason. You use up your childhood" (McCulloch and Simpson 244).

The problem of the relation between lived experience and fiction is complex, however, and it is entangled in the conflicting positions of *producer* and *citizen*. Munro's position on that issue is evident when she is asked by an interviewer for her views on "Initram," the story by her friend Audrey Thomas described in chapter 1. In that work, the unfolding story of the character Lydia becomes the focus of the narrative. It is common knowledge, in CanLit circles at least, that Lydia very closely resembles Alice Munro.

That Thomas's fiction is strongly autobiographical is well known, and Thomas herself appears to be questioning ideologies of literary invention when she opens this story with the words "Writers are terrible liars" and cheekily begins the next five paragraphs with the words "The truth is...." Fictive/autobiographical self-consciousness is foregrounded in this text: the narrator describes Lydia as telling a story; the overheard lovemaking at the end is "the last line in the last paragraph of the story [Lydia had] been writing all evening" (A. Thomas 106). The narrator herself is writing a story; she tells Lydia that she is "thinking of writing a story about her," even allowing the Munro-like character to choose her own fictional name; "I always wanted to be called Lydia," she says (107). The narrator's proposed title for this story is "Chicken Wings," but Lydia dislikes that title.

In her biography of Alice Munro, Catherine Sheldrick Ross flatly states that the details of Munro's marriage breakup are "depicted" in "Initram," and Munro does not disagree. She responds, "actually in that story, Audrey puts real things in and then she invents. The stuff about me having an orgasm in the next room is totally invented....But the chicken wings, the kind of dishes, the wine, the coming back home to cook, that was all true" (75). When questioned by Beverly Rasporich about the autobiographical elements in her own work, Munro compares herself to Audrey Thomas: "I think that there are writers who create out of their imaginations, but I am not one of them. I'm on the Audrey Thomas side of the fence, though I think I put them through more washes, you know, to bring them up" (23). The way an author constructs her own level of "fictiveness" is a useful way to understand her position-taking in the literary field, and Munro's uneasiness with the view of the author as recipient of the Muse's bounty is clear when she characterizes herself as "the opposite of a writer with a quick gift, you know, someone who gets it all piped in" (McCulloch and Simpson 239).

Another guide to Munro's fictive technique is to look at what is excluded from her oeuvre. In the case of *Who Do You Think You Are?*, one reason Munro gives for the abandonment of the Rose and Janet manuscript is its metafictionality—she found the structure of Janet as creator of Rose "too fancy...a little bit pretentious or precious" (Hoy 78). However, Munro does have a story very similar to "Initram," at least in its deployment of autobiography and metafiction. Though this story has appeared in print, it has never been collected, a fact that is certainly significant in Munro's self-construction as a writer. "Home" is a journal-like narrative of a woman writer's visit to her childhood home, to see her father and stepmother. Each journal entry is followed by an italicized passage in which the narrator debates with herself about how to tell the story, what to put in, what to leave out, what the tone should be. "I feel a bit treacherous and artificial," the narrator says, describing her reaction to the people of the community. She worries about the depiction of the stepmother, Irlma, a rough-edged character who describes the bowel movements of her dog in appalling detail. The narrator says, "I feel guilty about her, what I'm doing to her. Is this vengeful reporting, in spite of accuracy?" (149). The story ends, "I don't want any more effects, I tell you, lying. I want to do this with honour, if I possibly can" (153). Words like "honour" and "treacherous" indicate the dishonourable and treacherous position in which an author finds herself in dealing with the materials of her life and the tension between the demands of the field and her role as *citizen*.

But honour is also a useful word for a writer as a cultural worker who must not only interpret the culture she comes from, but honour the people it produces, by not treating them as so many pawns in a game of cool manipulation. In short, the ethical dilemmas of a Canadian woman short story writer are very evident here; not only does the field demand bad faith relative to the economy, but also bad faith in her relationships with others and with herself. Like Hugo in "Material" (see p. 98), the narrator of "Home" is asked to render coolly into Art the materials of her life, but she cannot help feeling treacherous in doing so. To cap this treachery with metafictional self-consciousness doubles the bind. In short, the story called "Home" shows how authorship creates a conflict between the producer and the citizen.

In her analysis of the Rose and Janet manuscript, Hoy says that "Rose and Janet is a more writerly collection than *Who Do You Think You Are?*, requiring more engagement in deciphering the silences" (72). Hoy asserts that Munro abandoned the manuscript because it was too metafictional, because it represented a "kind of deliberate cleverness to be eschewed" (78), that it was "too deliberate for Munro's aesthetic of indirection" (79). Munro's "aesthetic of indirection" is also incongruent with the novel form, and with the egotism of literary authority, which gives metafiction its cleverness. Hoy very rightly points out that, "In the collections after *Who Do You Think You Are?*, metafictional self-consciousness is less frequent and more buried; Munro looks less at the literal fictions to be made out of our lives and more at the extent to which lives are themselves already self-created fictions" (79). In effect, as Munro's authority with regard to genre grows, her work also moves steadily away from both the obviously autobiographical and the metafictional. In general, narrators are less present and the stories focus more on the strangeness, the uniqueness of individual characters. The "self-created fictions" of her characters' lives are comment enough on the problems of literary authority. Interestingly, the *Wingham Advance-Times* editorial immediately precedes the publication of *The Moons of Jupiter*, with its tales of the Chaddeleys and Flemings of "Dalgleish."

In 1976, Alice Munro and Margaret Laurence shared the dubious distinction of having their books banned in small-town Ontario. Laurence's *The Diviners* was removed from the grade 13 curriculum at Lakefield High School because of its sexual content, while in nearby Kenner, Munro's *Lives of Girls and Women* was banned for similar reasons. The experience was extremely painful for Laurence, but Munro remained more philosophical: "I though this was hilarious. It gave me a new lease on life, like being thought a scarlet woman. [Laurence] was a more serious person than I was, in the sense of her life in the world....She grew up in a small town. She should have known there's a lot of ill will" (Wainwright 143). Perhaps the geographical distance between Kenner and Clinton allowed Munro to find the banning "hilarious," but such "ill will" can be painful. Joyce Wayne describes the above-mentioned editorial in the *Wingham Advance-Times* as "both the heartbreak and strength of her writer's life" (9); when Munro describes an angry letter from a citizen of Wingham who asked "who do you think you are?," Wayne notes that Munro "laughs, but the humour is bittersweet" (10). However, as with the genre conflict in the production of *Who Do You Think You Are?*, Munro responds to the hometown editorial with strength: by reasserting her authority to write about Huron County in *The Moons of Jupiter* and in subsequent books, thus also reasserting her position as cultural producer.

The subtext of the metafictional, autobiographical, and treacherous story called "Initram" is that writers *are* terrible liars—in both senses of the word. In effect, Thomas lies terribly—meaning inadequately, ineptly—in "Initram." In her own work, Munro lies terribly in the other sense of the word, as in more skilfully, more adeptly. Though Munro uses autobiographical material, she puts her characters through "a few more washes, to bring them up." She writes/lies "better" than Thomas—meaning more fictively, more imaginatively (not "better" in a qualitative sense)—and in so doing lies more terribly, is even more treacherous. It is in her confidence (and skill) as producer that Munro is able to withstand attacks on her citizenship arising from the "ill will" of the small town.

The issue of autobiography, which is traditionally rated as a lesser genre, comes into play here as well. There is an intriguing point, shortly after the publication of *Who Do You Think You Are?*, when the question of memoir is raised by Munro's American cultural bankers. Archival correspondence from Virginia Barber and Ann Close suggests that, following the generic struggles over *Who Do You Think You Are?*, Munro, in league with her agent and publisher's editor, is contemplating a generic shift to "memoir" and that, at the early draft stages, stories including "The Moons of Jupiter" and "Dulse" (collected in the 1982 *The Moons of Jupiter*) as well as "Working for a Living" (uncollected, but published in *Grand Street* 1.1 (Autumn 1981): 9-37) were generically classified as memoir by the three. The attraction of memoir is that it can mean "book," which means "bulk," which suggests "novel," which means "marketable," and possibly avoids the last-minute wrangles of the previous collection. However, the appearance of the editorial in the Wingham paper coincides with the final preparations for this fifth book, and could have been a deciding factor in her choosing the label of fiction over memoir. As Noah Richler comments in his article on memoirs by the children of writers, "Writing is an act of betrayal—if you're any good at it, that is. Better to keep it to folk you can pretend you don't know." (B5)

Besides, in terms of the hierarchy of genres available to the producer, memoir falls even lower than the short story. As Helen Buss remarks, "Traditionally, autobiography is considered a lesser art than fiction by those who make and break literary canons, and as many creative writers well know, to admit the autobiographical nature of one's work is, to some minds, equivalent to admitting to being an amateur" (5). The generic choice of memoir, for Munro, presents the risk of "losing class" in the "hierarchically structured space" (Bourdieu, *Field* 95) of the literary field, and ultimately, Munro and her two cultural bankers discard the idea of memoir, despite its book-like potential. In reaction to both the possibility of outraged citizenry and genre risk, therefore, Munro's next collection, *The Moons of Jupiter,* is pointedly advertised and marketed as "stories"; the flap copy comments on how "the stories always ring true, because of Alice Munro's way with her characters, or, more precisely, her people." The word "story" or "stories" is used six times in the jacket blurb. Whatever the "truth" value of the works, and whether they describe "characters" or "people," there is no doubt that these are works of fiction. A disclaimer appears on the copyright page—the usual "All characters in this book are fictitious and any resemblance to persons living or dead is coincidental." Such a disclaimer has appeared in every one of Munro's published texts, from *Lives of Girls and Women* onwards.[5]

Because writers are subjects in cultural ideology, their work must conform to or uphold certain systems of belief prevalent in their culture. Thomas Docherty remarks the "close analogy between the aesthetic and political dispositions" (58). In general, Munro's sense of social direction allows her to adhere well to rules that are entrenched as "aesthetic" requirements, masking their connection to the larger ideologies of politics, power, economics, race, gender, and class. Frank Davey shows how the development of the literary reputation of the short story was in part a process of differentiating it from religious tract or fairy tale ("Genre" 138). By the late twentieth century, the modern short story eschews "moral advice" or a "message." Ours is a secular culture in which religious or spiritual solutions to human dilemmas are seen, at best, as empty proselytizing and, at worst, as insidious mind control, and certainly, in Munro's work, spiritual questions remain unanswerable. Characters who embrace religion, whether traditional or fundamentalist or New Age, are generally seen as victims, as misguided.[6] The secular culture of the twentieth century demands of its literature a reflection of its own mistrust of spiritual solutions to real human dilemmas, not as an aesthetic matter but as an ideological one. However, literary culture tends to posit itself, Art, as the only proper answer to the spiritual quest, finding in this ideological requirement the opportunity to advertise itself as redemptive.

The elision of the political, the collective, the communal, is another important aspect of humanist literary ideology. Citing Terry Eagleton's characterization of literature as "the vanishing point of the political," Sarah King comments that "In other words, the literary *is* political, although its success depends on concealing this identification" (7). Contemporary fiction tends to focus on the struggles of an individual to achieve self-realization; in general, family ties, communities, systems of belief, and, often, marriages are to be examined, explored, found wanting, and discarded in the struggle for financial, moral, and often artistic independence. Lennard Davis has said of the classic realist mode that "one thing the novel finds almost impossible to describe is collective action....Given the requirements of creating a recognizable and easily distinguished character in novels, individuality is clearly going to be given a very high priority" (119). Davis's argument centres very much on the novel, but his point about individualism applies even more aptly to the short story. With its necessary limitations of time and space, the short story finds it difficult to accommodate the concerns of more than one character.

The political is obviously elided in Munro's fiction; racism is muted in "Day of the Butterfly," and Munro has been exceedingly cautious about making overt feminist statements or espousing feminist activism throughout her career. For example, in "A Queer Streak" from *The Progress of Love*, the central character,

Violet, is visited by her niece and a young friend. The young women are "dressed up in army outfits" (333) and are "generally thought to be women's libbers" (335). Following their visit, the women send Violet a card, thanking her for discussing her personal history with them. Their note reads: "It is a classic story of anti-patriarchal rage....What is called Female Craziness is nothing but centuries of Frustration and Oppression" (339). The note is bewildering to the elderly Violet and equally puzzling to her nephew Dane, whose lifelong relationship with Violet has now become a caretaking role. Often, feminist dogma is seen as an amusing irrelevance to the complex lives of Munro characters.

Even social class structures are usually viewed from the quirky viewpoint of a single, often artistic individual. Munro has published very little non-fiction prose, but what has appeared is markedly more political than her collected fiction. For example, her only published critical essay on another's work is a piece called "Remember Roger Mortimer," a nostalgic look at Dickens's *A Child's History of England.* Munro describes her childhood enjoyment of these lurid tales of political and romantic intrigue, but her concluding lines question the complacent assurance of the Victorian writer. She comments that, to the Victorians, "Things are not perfect, perhaps they never will be, but it is impossible not to believe in the shining reality of Progress, and to see that men are slowly becoming more civilized, more rational and humane, so that their greatest mistakes, their greatest insanities and brutalities must surely lie in the past. I remember the summer I read this....It was 1939" (37). Likewise, when commissioned to research and write a historical piece for a television series called *The Newcomers* in 1979, Munro produced "A Better Place Than Home" to describe the inhumane treatment of Irish immigrants attempting to escape the famine of 1847. In the story of a young Irish Catholic couple, Munro's political statements are more overt than those found in her fiction. She describes signs in the windows of workplaces saying "No Irish or Dogs," and the dialogue of workers who have not received their promised wages but dare not complain: "Raise a fuss and in comes the military and they end up going to jail.

Then they write it up in the paper and they call it a riot. They never call it a strike, they call it a riot. They always say it was the drink done it; they never mention the wages" (121). These two pieces outside Munro's "body of work" show the larger world of social injustice, history, bigotry, and capitalist greed as a far stronger presence than in her collected fiction. In "Carried Away" from *Open Secrets*, for example, the librarian's ghostly encounter with her lost love occurs during a ceremony commemorating the Tolpuddle Martyrs, early trade unionists. Yet when Louisa hears Jack Agnew says "Love never dies," her reaction is cynical: "She felt impatient to the point of taking offense. This is what all the speechmaking turns you into, she thought, a person who can say things like that" (48).

Certainly, in Munro's later work the sociohistorical takes on a greater weight than in the highly personal and individually focused stories of love, family, and loss in the first half of her writing career, but as Lennard Davis points out: "As part of the general ideology of middle-class individualism, the idea that the subject might be formed from social forces and that change might have to come about through social change is by and large absent" from fiction (119). This is certainly true of the vast majority of Munro's work—except that, as is the tendency with literary fiction, the bias is *against* middle-class values and *for* artistic freedom/individualism. Once again, I stress that this analysis does not critique Munro for failing to agitate for social change in her short stories; instead, these examples serve to show how Munro, as producer, astutely "reads" the ideology of the field and thus ensures her right to speak. In short, by observing the literary/ideological rules of the field, Munro gains the authority to subtly question the status quo in her fiction, especially as it relates to nationality, gender, genre, and class. Despite the "dominated" position of the artist, and the fact that "distances are prudently maintained" between the cultural and the political in the field, Bourdieu remarks that "cultural producers are able to use the power conferred on them, especially in periods of crisis, by their capacity to put forward a critical definition of the social world, to mobilize the potential strength of the dominated classes and subvert the order prevailing in the field of power" (*Field* 43).

One example of Munro's subtlety in this area is in the way the issue of race is muted in the early story "Day of the Butterfly." As has been noted, this story is modernist in form, and a part of its modernism is its refusal of polemic. Myra's ostracism is never overtly ascribed to her racial difference. However, the author gives a few tantalizing details that suggest that Myra's "difference" is in fact racial: her voice was "the lightest singsong" (*Dance* 100); Myra and her brother had "long smooth oval faces...dark, oily, shining hair" (101); Myra's hair is worn in long coiled braids "*as if* she was wearing a turban too big for her" (101; my emphasis); she has a "brown hand" (105) and a "brown carved face" (110). Despite these clues, the ethnicity and country of origin of the family are never given. The *Chatelaine* artist who provided the illustration for an earlier version of the story interpreted Myra's ethnicity as South Asian, at least to the eyes of this observer. However, critics and readers of "Day of the Butterfly" read Myra as an "Italian immigrant girl" (Polk 104) or as the child of "Eastern European immigrants...Roman Catholic" (Thacker, "Clear" 43). As an experiment, I gave this story to three different but equally astute readers of my own acquaintance and asked them to name Myra's country or region of origin. I got three different responses: Eastern Europe, the Middle East, and India. The antipolemic stance of the modern short story, while masquerading as an aesthetic quality, does in fact function as a suppressant of political resistance, yet, by personalizing the experience of subtle Canadian systemic racism through the eyes of a single white child, Munro formulates a resistance to or at least a questioning of that "othering" in a non-polemical form. In terms of Munro's questioning of gender roles and choices, I can personally attest to the transformative power of a reading of *Lives of Girls and Women* at the age of nineteen: I remember thinking, "Yes! Exactly! I want men to love me *and* I want to think about the universe when I look at the moon!" (see *LGW* 150). My reaction has been echoed in countless conversations with other women readers of Munro's work.

The ideological position of the author on the secular and the political effectively mirrors that of the society in which he or she writes, but one area in which the author in literary culture departs from the repression of comment on the political status quo is in his/her position on the issue of social class. It is the norm in popular fiction for characters to aspire to and achieve middle-class status or better. The characters in novels by Judith Krantz and Sidney Sheldon usually begin in poverty and move up to a life of designer fashions and worldly success. This pattern is less common in literary fiction, a phenomenon examined by Bourdieu:

> It is significant that the appearance of an anonymous "bourgeois" public, and the irruption of methods or techniques borrowed from the economic order, such as collective production or advertising for cultural products, coincides with the rejection of bourgeois aesthetics and with the methodical attempt to distinguish the artist and the intellectual from other commoners by positing the unique products of "creative genius" against interchangeable products, utterly and completely reducible to their commodity value. (*Field* 114)

Thus Bourdieu suggests that because one facet of the "charismatic" view of authorship is the denial or repression of the economic, then, as authorship borrows more from the economic order and its goods acquire more real value, it must distinguish itself ideologically from its bourgeois public by, among other things, a disdain for bourgeois values. Certainly, Munro's self-definition as a person of the lower class serves to legitimize her claim to the subject position of restricted producer. In interviews, she speaks openly of her childhood years in a "rural slum" (C. Ross 23). On the other hand, such a self-construction is problematic in terms of her position as *product* in a complex class system in which she is less glamorous than more popular writers, and certainly poorer than the patrons of the arts who purchase tables for a "cultural benefit." In effect, the assumption of a particular class position has both advantages and drawbacks.

A disdain for the bourgeois is a particular marker of the field
of restricted production, that is, the field of high as opposed to
popular art. In Munro's authorship, the tension between seriousness and popularity is evident. But her status as cultural producer in the restricted field as opposed to the field of large-scale
production is complicated by her Canadian-ness. Munro herself
says it best, describing her reaction when a fellow author on the
"Chinada"[7] trip described her as a popular writer:

> I was upset because I think I am a serious writer. But I was
> also surprised to think that I was thought of as a popular
> writer. Because I think of someone who sells millions of
> books, like Harold Robbins, as a popular writer. Then I
> thought about it and decided that anyone who makes a living
> in Canada is probably a popular writer. And therefore you
> must accept that you cater to the popular taste in some way
> unbeknownst to yourself. (Hancock 198)

Munro makes a valid point here. Though her position-taking in
the field is that of a "serious" or "restricted" producer, the small
size of the Canadian market makes any modestly successful
Canadian author "popular" in a sense. When a new Munro collection appears, it *is* reviewed in the popular press, but is also
extensively treated in scholarly journals and theses, and frequently anthologized and taught in undergraduate and graduate
courses. Though Munro's fiction is certainly not avant-garde, it
*is* taken seriously by the academy in a way that other "popular"
Canadian writers such as Constance Beresford-Howe or L.R.
Wright or William Deverell are not. However, her "seriousness"
extends to the larger market of the United States and Britain as
well, as her *New Yorker* affiliation, her Booker nominations, and
reviews of her work in the *New York Times Book Review* and the
*Times Literary Supplement* attest. What is crucial in her self-construction as restricted producer, however, is that any catering to
the public taste is accidental, "unbeknownst."

In any case, Munro certainly appears to participate quite com-
fortably in the general disdain for bourgeois culture typical of
works coming from the field of restricted production. Awareness
of class is particularly strong in *Who Do You Think You Are?*, the

pivotal work of Munro's position-taking in the cultural field. Rose marries Patrick in hopes of finding fulfillment in material comfort and financial security, only to end up as a divorced struggling artist, but with her integrity intact. In *For Openers*, Alan Twigg comments that Rose "is never allowed to get anything. She's always unfulfilled" (19), to which Munro responds: "She gets something. She gets herself. She doesn't get the obvious things, the things she think she wants....She gets a knowledge of herself" (19). What Munro characters think they want is what society tells them they should want—marriage, security, love, family—but what they get instead is the individualistic ideal of self-knowledge and independence. Rose's disdain for the bourgeois smugness of her brother Brian, and for the crass materialism and moral laxity of her friends Clifford and Jocelyn, is indicative of the way in which literary culture disdains the materialistic pretension and complacency of the bourgeoisie in order to differentiate itself and its practitioners from its audience, to place itself apart from and above its anonymous public. Bourdieu links this disdain to the author's proprietary relationship with language; he remarks that "the best indicator of the autonomy of the field of restricted production [is] the disjunction between its own principles of evaluation and those that the 'general public'—and especially the non-intellectual fraction of the dominant class—applies to its productions" (*Field* 116). Thus, says Bourdieu, "individual production must be oriented towards the search for culturally pertinent features endowed with value in the field's own economy. This confers properly cultural value on the producers by endowing them with marks of distinction (a specialty, a manner, a style)" (117). In other words, an author's "style," her "vividness" in uses of language, is a marker of her artistic autonomy and thus legitimacy. If the author "owns" language in this way, then bourgeois judgments of her work can be dismissed and even disdained. However, one problem with this system of belief is that bourgeois culture, particularly the academy, is the producer of the consumers of literature. As Bourdieu remarks, the field of restricted production has a "profound dependence on the educational system, the indispensable means of its reproduction and growth" (123) in the sense that the educational system produces the audience for works in the restricted field. Whereas "consumption in the field of large-scale production is more or less independent of the educational level of consumers,...works of restricted art owe their specifically cultural rarity, and thus their function as elements of social distinction, to the rarity of the instruments with which they may be deciphered" (120).

Literary culture thus places the writer in a problematic relation with her own reading public, and especially in her relationship with the academy. In an article called "The Functions of Literature," Michel Foucault describes the relationship between the artist and the academy as an increasingly close one since the nineteenth century to the point that, these days, "literature functions as literature through an interplay of selection, sacralization and institutional validation, of which the university is both the operator and the receiver" (308-309). As Laurence Mathews has suggested, the relationship between academy and author in Canada is even closer than that in other Western cultures, because of the relative youth of CanLit, in which literary works are canonized in "the simultaneous embracing of a work by the classroom and the academic journal" (155). According to Mathews, "in Canada, it is a relatively small group that makes the decisions about what books are fit for canonization: university teachers of English who specialize or dabble in Canadian literature" (155). In the twentieth century, Foucault says, "so-called avant-garde literature is read only by university teachers and their students," and furthermore, "writers live mainly by teaching and lecturing" (308-9), to the extent that the two institutions—the academy and the literary field—once "profoundly linked, [now] tended to merge completely" (308-309).

However, the merger is an uneasy one. Bourdieu remarks, for example, on how producers are "embittered by that type of teacher, the *lector*, who comments on and explains the work of others...and whose own production owes much to the professional practice of its author and to the position he or she occupies within the system of production and circulation of symbolic goods" (*Field* 124). An instance of this "embitterment" is evident in a non-fiction piece by Munro called "The Colonel's Hash Resettled," in which she complains about a critic who said that, in her story "Images," "the house in the ground—the roofed-over cellar that the hermit lives in—symbolized death, of course, and burial, and that it was a heavy gloomy sort of story because there was nothing to symbolize resurrection" (181). Munro protests that she in fact intended nothing of the sort, that the house in the ground is no more than a house in the ground, an actual house remembered from her childhood. She asks, "Surely a roofed-over cellar doesn't mean any such thing...unless I want it to? Surely it's not that simple? I wrote the story, didn't I? If I hadn't sat down and written the story he wouldn't be able to talk about it, and come to all these interesting and perhaps profitable conclusions about Canadian literature" (181). Munro struggles with a variety of ambivalences here: about academic critics who presume to know more about her work than she does, about such critics making a profit on their assessments of her work, about these critiques of her work being turned into statements about Canadian literature.

However, having pondered the dilemma, Munro indicates how she is caught between belief systems by drawing the conclusion that "What you write is an offering; anybody can come and take what they like from it" (181). Nonetheless, this bothers Munro, remembering the real house from which the fictional one is drawn: "I have somehow betrayed it, putting it in a story to be extracted this way, as a bloodless symbol. There is a sort of treachery to innocent objects—to houses, chairs, dresses, dishes, and to roads, fields, landscapes—which a writer removes from their natural, dignified obscurity and sets down in print" (181-82). This sentiment about the betrayal of inanimate objects of course echoes the narrator's objection to the fictionalization of human lives in "Material" or "Home" and indicates Munro's awareness that such "betrayal" leaves her open to attacks such as that in the *Wingham Advance-Times* editorial. In other words, her work as a producer compromises her position as citizen.

Bourdieu insists that the study of the cultural producer must include not only "the sociology he produces," but also "the sociology of which he is the object" (160). In the sociology of which Munro is the object, therefore, lived experience and autobiography, metafiction and modernism, the secular and the political, canonization and the academy all combine in various ways, creating a complex of belief systems that combine and contend within the "plurality of selves" known as "author."

In "Literature and Biography" (1923), Boris Tomashevsky asserts that "the biography that is useful to the literary historian is not the author's *curriculum vitae* or the investigator's account of his life. What the literary historian really needs is the biographical legend created by the author himself. Only such a legend is a *literary fact*" (89). This study has so far questioned investigators' accounts such as those presented in biographies like Ross's *A Double Life* and biographical sketches like Bennett's and Brown's. If I do not seek Munro in her texts or in the accounts of other investigators, then what kind of legend do I see Munro creating for herself in her self-construction as "writer"?

Munro has said that in her early married life, she knew that her peers would scorn her literary ambitions, so when she did go down to the basement to write, she pretended to be making curtains instead (C. Ross 55). She has commented that "Writing's something I did, like the ironing" ("Writing's Something I Did" E1). When asked by an interviewer to describe her "fictional aesthetic," Munro laughs and says, "You know very well I haven't got such a thing" (Hancock 189). Her remarks on influence are similar: "I'm not interested in any literary tradition. I read things that I enjoy, that nourish me. But I never seem to put things together" (Hancock 188). Thus Munro deliberately constructs her authorship as non- or anti-academic.

On the other hand, describing a story she dislikes because it is imitative, she comments that "the tone of it is not *felt*. The tone of it is assumed. It's a trick" (Struthers, "Real" 23), thereby suggesting that the role of producer must be approached honourably, honestly, with an awareness of one's citizenship in the world. From these comments and others previously noted, a portrait emerges of a woman who is uneasy with the ways in which culture authorizes writers, and who is keenly aware of the conflicts between the author's positions as product, producer, and citizen.

These ideological tensions are visible in the archive, particularly in correspondence with Barber, Close, and Metcalf. Examples of Munro's shyness and reluctance to play the public role recur throughout her archive. Though I am not permitted to quote from such letters, Munro's unease with the notion of author as product, as a position that engenders in her a sense of unreality, is evident from correspondence found in both her archive and Metcalf's. The problem is partly rooted in the writer's complex relationship with the academy, without whose "consecration" she cannot be construed a "serious" writer, and the concomitant yet contradictory need to market her work to the public in order to make a living.

On the most basic level, the correspondence files reveal the demands that the academy and the publishing business make on the writer's time. A tabulation of the contents of correspondence dated 1980 through 1985 indicates that the majority of letters Munro receives take the form of requests—for readings, personal appearances, and book jacket quotes, as well as invitations to literary events, conferences, and panels. Established authors write to ask Munro to provide references for their grant applications; unpublished writers ask Munro to comment on their work and dispense publication advice. Universities offer writer-in-residence positions and visiting professorships; various organizations ask the author to donate signed copies of her work, or to donate time or money to various causes.

The Munro archive contains seventy-five requests for readings, performances, or personal appearances between 1980 and 1985. (This statistic obviously does not include invitations and requests not collected in the archive, or discarded, or received in person or by phone. I would suspect that an accounting of all such requests would probably double the number.) If she accepted each one, she'd be making a public appearance every three to four weeks. Some of these are unpaid appearances in support of various causes, but the majority offer "a small honorarium" plus travel expenses and accommodation. Honoraria range from $200 to $1000, but the low end of the scale is more common. Twelve "blurbs" are solicited, and sixteen people, ranging from high school students to established scholars, request a personal interview. Academic invitations include fourteen conferences or panels, nine visiting professorships, and four writer-in-residence posts. Part of Munro's durability as an author appears to stem from her self-protectiveness, her insistence on allowing herself the private space and time to write. In this regard, she is unlike her contemporary, Margaret Laurence, who, by many accounts, was unable to produce another novel after 1974's *The Diviners* because she simply stretched herself too thin. Patricia Morley describes a form letter composed by Laurence in 1980, "giving notice that she cannot undertake to do any of the following: read manuscripts; write book reviews; provide quotes for book jackets; give readings or conduct seminars; participate in writer's workshops or panels; give advice on essays or theses; provide photographs, biographical information or copies of her books; receive visitors, attend conferences, give interviews or appear on television or radio; give speeches, lectures or graduation addresses; judge writing contests; or reply personally to readers' letters" (155). Morley notes, however, that "the warning was hollow" and that Laurence continued her political and environmental activism, her battles against censorship, and her warm support of "the tribe" of upcoming and established Canadian writers, until her death from cancer in 1987.

The practical demands made by literary culture on an established writer's time are only one aspect of the problem, however. Perhaps even more difficult is the ideological problem of the work, and even the writer herself, as product. In short, a writer requires an audience, but the demands of promotion undermine the writer's integrity. Andrew Wernick defines promotion as "any act or process of communication that serves to stimulate the circulation of something in the context of its competitive exchange" (88). However, because of the laws of the field of restricted cultural production, and of the inverse relationship between symbolic capital and market capital, the requirement of promotion creates "problems for intellectual and artistic producers which exceed those usually ascribed to commercialism" (88). Part of Munro's response to these problems, as with the problem of demands on her time, is in constructing herself as publicity-shy. Certainly, correspondence from Ann Close at Knopf shows how the planning for the promotion of *The Moons of Jupiter* takes into account Munro's ambivalence about her public role (e.g., Acc. 396/87.3 Box 1 File 3). What exactly do these public appearances take out of the writer? Apparently, they create in her a sense of unreality, grounded in the way the literary field is characterized by "an opposition between small-scale and large-scale (commercial) production, i.e. between the primacy of production and the field of producers or even the sub-field of producers for producers, and the primacy of marketing, audience, sales and success measured quantitatively" (Bourdieu, *Field* 82).

Academic consecration poses a similar "opposition" in that academic recognition seems to promote an aura of unreality as well. Catherine Sheldrick Ross was a junior faculty member when Munro served as writer-in-residence at the University of Western Ontario in 1974-75. Ross observes that Munro "found the public role emotionally draining and almost fraudulent" (77). In the *Paris Review* interview, Munro remarks on the irony that "The only things that ever stopped me from writing were the jobs—when I was defined publicly as a writer and given an office to work in" (McCulloch and Simpson 251). According to Frank Davey, the common mode of production in the nineteenth and twentieth centuries is that of "capitalist novelists who work for a publisher, receive payment for their copyright, write in accessible language, and rely on long-press-run distribution"; however, notes Davey, in Canadian literary culture, "The universities, through their tenure and promotion policies, have in this century created another possibility [for authorial position-taking]: the writer who writes for a small, educated audience, is rewarded not by royalties or stipends but by university position, who writes in relatively complex combinations of genres, and who relies on short-run distribution by literary or academic presses" ("Writers" 101).

Such authorial types occupy a subfield of the restricted field—but this is an area that Munro has resisted, for reasons explainable by her long-term suspicion of academe as well as by her sense of marginalization in terms of gender, class, and genre. For example, the archival correspondence contains several offers of writer-in-residence positions. A 1982 letter from Sam Solecki at the University of Toronto is particularly instructive in its metaphoric implications. As with many correspondents who seem to know that Munro must be approached with caution, Solecki presents his case apologetically, offering the writer the option of a full-time or part-time position. This is obviously not Solecki's first attempt; his letter concludes, "I begin to feel like a suitor who has been rejected more times than he cares to remember" (Acc. 396/87.3 Box 2 File 1).[8] Certainly, for Munro, many aspects of the public role of writer resemble an unwanted suitor whose advances she must reject in order to maintain her virtue. One of the ironies of the field, for Bourdieu, is that the autonomy of producers in the restricted field is located in "an *auctoritas* that recognize[s] no other principle of legitimation than itself." Thus such producers "cannot but resist...the institutional authority which the educational system, as a consecratory institution, opposes to their competing claims" (*Field* 124). These "competing claims" are evident in the archival correspondence: in 1983, a representative from Mount Holyoke College writes to Munro, asking her to evaluate the fiction of a female academic up for a tenure-track position (Acc. 396/87.3 Box 1 File 15). The request evokes the image of a snake eating its own tail: the academy canonizes the author in a manner that opposes her "entire practice, [her] entire professional ideology" (Bourdieu 124), then asks her to participate in the selection of the next generation of canon-makers. Considering the ambivalent relation between the author and the academy, such a request is laden with irony.

Munro's personal correspondence is not among her archival papers; she resists the construction of author as product by excising the personal from her archive as well as by refusing or being reluctant to play the the public role. However, the col-

lected papers of John Metcalf are also held at the University of
Calgary, and Metcalf, unlike Munro, is neither reticent nor self-
protective, a man obviously comfortable with his public role.
One box of his vast archive unearths a voluminous, intimate, and
heartfelt epistolary friendship with the poet John Newlove, an
extensive literary/philosophical dialogue with Simon Fraser professor and writer John Mills, an astute and kindly mentoring of
a young immigrant writer named Rohinton Mistry, and a warm
and mutually supportive correspondence with Alice Munro. The
Munro-Metcalf correspondence is different from, say, the
Newlove-Metcalf file, both in its relative size and personal depth,
but the friendship between Metcalf and Munro is obvious. My
discussion focuses on Metcalf's responses to letters from
Munro, written between 1980 and 1988, photocopies of which
are part of Metcalf's own archive.

The Munro-Metcalf correspondence demonstrates peer support, a good dash of literary gossip, and a picture of how these
two understand their social role. In his letters, Metcalf is warmly
supportive of and complimentary to Munro. Munro's construction of Metcalf as an ally in the struggle against the academy is
evident when she describes receiving a letter from Metcalf,
praising an early story, possibly "Images." Munro had recently
received a devastating critique of her work from a professor at
the University of Victoria, and she recalls that Metcalf's support
helped her to regain her confidence (Acc. 396/87.3 Box 6 File 6).
This was the beginning of a mutually supportive friendship that
endured for many years. For example, on hearing that Munro
sensed a bias against fiction writers at a literary gathering,
Metcalf leaps to her defence: "One paragraph of your stories is
more poetic than ____ and ____ squared. How dare they give
themselves airs?" (MsC 24.8.9.3). On 9 May 1982, Metcalf writes,
"By the way, I read your story in *Atlantic* and thought it was a
real knock-out. You're getting better and better all the time. It's
depressing. You're also getting more *mysterious*" (MsC 24.8.9.5).
However, when Metcalf asks for her opinion of a recent story, he
does so cautiously, apparently anticipating that Munro will be
uncomfortable with the request. In some ways, part of Munro's

discomfort is with the romantic notion of the "godlike" author. In her commentary in the 1970 Metcalf anthology *Sixteen by Twelve*, Munro discusses the relationship between her own history and the role of writer: "When I started to write the dreadful things I did write when I was about fifteen, I made the glorious leap from being a victim of my own ineptness and self-conscious miseries to being a godlike arranger of patterns and destinies, even if they were all in my head" (125). Although Munro asserts the romantic author-god notion in this public space, in the letters of the archive she appears somewhat more tentative. On the whole, Metcalf wears his authority far more easily than Munro. As well, Munro, after two or three decades of ideological struggle with biases of nationality, gender, genre, and class, may be finding that the "godlike" control writing offered her at fifteen is now severely compromised by the realities of the cultural field.

Metcalf is a powerful figure in Canadian literature as well; his list of anthology publications is almost as long as Weaver's (see appendix 2). The difference is, though, that he is a peer, of sorts. In accepting Munro's critique of his story, his initial response is mildly defensive, polite: "Many thanks, Alice, for thinking about the story. As always, I value what you say" (MsC 24.8.9.17.f3). Shortly thereafter, however, he writes again to confess that he has decided to take her critical advice: "I've been brooding about what you said about the first section...and—damn you—have decided that you were not totally without reason and justice so I'm cutting out about 2 1/2 pages—maybe more" (MsC 24.8.9.18).

Another powerful indication of the gender gap in the authorial field is Metcalf's extreme openness about his private life and opinions. The difference between the Metcalf and Munro archives in terms of the willingness to expose the personal is arresting. As a white, middle-class male with some education and considerable canonizing power as an anthologist, Metcalf has no qualms about passing public judgments on his fellow writers. His letters to Munro devote a fair amount of the dialogue to CanLit gossip about who wore what inappropriate costume to a literary event, or how badly this person read, or how poorly executed that person's fiction is. Metcalf is widely known (and feared) for his reputation as a scathing satirist and his disruptive and pugnacious persona. The comparison between the two archives reminds one of Munro's remark that a man can be outrageous in public in ways for which a woman would not be forgiven. And indeed, it's difficult not to laugh at some of Metcalf's more outrageous remarks, such as "When ____ ____ took over PEN, I felt prompted *to defend torture*" (MsC 24.8.9.f1). Munro is far more subdued in her remarks, though not immune to resentments and competitive aggressions. However, a stark illustration of Munro's fear of being unforgiven is the fact that she herself generally deletes the names of her intended victims from her letters, while in Metcalf's case, I have done him that service, as much for my own protection as for his.

Letters between Munro and Metcalf in 1988 (MsC. 24.8.9. 24, 25) reveal the strong relationship between the construction of the author as artificer and the problematic relationship of that artifice to the autobiographical. Metcalf's responses to Munro's scepticism about the confessional work of another author provide an illustration of what Bourdieu describes as "conflicts between agents occupying different positions in the production of products of the same type" (79): "Even if these struggles never clearly set the 'commercial' against the 'non-commercial,' 'distinterestedness' against 'cynicism,' they almost always involve recognition of the ultimate values of 'disinterestedness' through the denunciation of the mercenary compromises or calculating manoeuvres of the adversary" (79). The actual truth value of what this other author says is undermined, for Munro, by the use of autobiography as an opportunity for personal advancement, attention, worldy recognition, possibly even sympathy. In short, the material is untrue *aesthetically*.

In a commentary on "Boys and Girls" in his anthology *New Worlds*, Metcalf says that the story rings "*true*, whether Alice Munro invented the detail or not" (9). In the modern short story, autobiographical truth is beside the point; it's the "aesthetic" truth that matters. This position is intrinsic to the ideology of the field of restricted production. For a writer like Munro, an author undermines her credibility by opportunistically catering to the market; thus as a producer, this author has surrendered "autonomy." As Andrew Wernick remarks, an author is doubly implicated both as "operator of a (self-)promotional practice" and "(via the imaging and publicizing of a name) as a produced promotional sign" (88), thus creating a situation in which "the well of authenticity is poisoned at the source" (90).

Interestingly, Metcalf's take on this confessional author moves in a misogynist direction, when he describes his own experience of a reading by this same author: "it was *awful*—but worse, it was all nothing but ill-written *journalism*. And worse than that, the audience, 98% women, were all damp of eye and the general feeling was of a secular tent-meeting where at any moment people would have confessed or torn any males present limb from limb" (MsC 24.8.9.25.f 1-2). Thus, while Munro's uneasiness centres on the violation of certain authorial principles, Metcalf tends to read the problem as gender-based, tying in the "aesthetic" judgment of "journalistic" writing to the political problem of feminist outrage.

That Munro views the cultural demands of authorship as a threat to her safety as a writer is clear in a letter to Metcalf in which she expresses her frustration at the way in which the necessity of doing public authorial functions makes it difficult to maintain the necessary creative space for writing (MsC. 24.8.9.1). Metcalf commiserates, "of course I understand. And especially about not feeling 'in' writing. For me, each new story is a voyage into impossibility" (MsC 24.8.9.11).

Munro's strong sense of social direction has guided her to this increasingly authoritative position in the field, but the simultaneous repression of the economic, coupled with the requirement of promotion, places her in a difficult position. The promotion, the public role, "feels" wrong for Munro, when compared to how she views her own practice, her own work.

Bourdieu has remarked that "Entering the field of literature is not so much like going into a religion as getting into a select club" (*Field* 77), a club defined according to norms that seem inauthentic, even antithetical, to Munro's self-construction and practice. Munro senses that she does not belong in this "select club," not only because of her gender but also because she is nonintellectual, because she is of "lower caste," and because she is operating at an intuitive level that, of course, does not fit with the modernist definition of impersonal artificer following a great tradition.

Certainly, Munro's insecurities about whether she belongs in this club, and also whether she wants to belong—in an environment in which women are subject to both sanctification and scorn (MsC. 24.8.9.22, 24)—are couched in terms of how the public role of writer, with its necessities of academic canonization and commercial promotion, destroys what is real and praiseworthy in an author's work—how it threatens, undermines, and makes fraudulent the "real" individual, the "real" woman writer. Becoming an "author," for Munro, is to betray what it is to be the "writer" that she is. Certainly, from her early hiding of writing activities in basements to her continuing intimidation in the face of cultural promotion and academic credentials, she is, in some ways, placed in the position of "beggar maid," the female outsider with a poverty of correct credentials for the claim of authorship.

## CHAPTER VI

## "CONCLUSION"
# What Is a Canadian Woman Short Story Author?

The literary world has sunk to a new low. The book [*The Beggar Maid*] contained more gutter language than I have ran across [*sic*] in a long time. I found no redeeming qualities whatever in the book. In my opinion its [*sic*] nothing but a cesspool of filth. And to think I had to pay good money for it. I would sell it back to you for a nickel."

— undated letter to Alice Munro
   from a reader in St. Louis, Missouri

(MsC 38.2.74.4)

---

Notes for chapter 6 are on p. 176.

What makes a writer an author? Foucault has noted that "in our culture, the name of an author is a variable that accompanies only certain texts to the exclusion of others" ("Author" 267); for example, a letter, contract, or poster may have a writer, but not an author. The ideological formation of the two terms is evident in these dictionary definitions:

> Author: 1. One who produces, creates or brings into being; the beginner, creator, or first mover of anything. 2. One who composes and writes books, or whose occupation is to compose or write books.

> Writer: a person whose business or occupation is writing; specifically, a) a copyist; a scribe or clerk; b) an author, journalist or the like. (*Webster's New Twentieth Century Dictionary*, Unabridged, 1978).

The gap between these two titles centres on the way in which "writer" is described as a "business" or "occupation"—that is, *process*—while "author" is defined in terms of results, of something being *produced*, such as a book. I, for example, am a "writer," of short stories and journals, and of letters, grocery lists, and admonishments to my children, but I am not an "author" unless the writing I do takes the form of a tangible object—such as a book—that has monetary and symbolic value. Thus, a "writer" can be anything from a humble scribe, copyist, or even journalist, or she can take the exalted place of "author" if she is, unlike a copyist, scribe, or journalist, 1) the *creator* of the "original" work, thus bringing in the romantic notion of the author as inspired genius or godlike creator; or 2) the *producer* of an object with tangible value in the real world. Munro's texts (*and* her grocery lists!) have a cash and cultural value—to most of her readers, at least; my grocery lists do not. The distinction, then, is partly one of process over product. Ironically, an author who successfully produces and promotes her literary products in effect becomes a product herself, a situation that legitimately gives rise to the sense of fraudulence or unreality evident in Munro's view of her public role.

But there's more to it than that. Nancy Hartsock, in her introduction to *Money, Sex and Power*, raises the intriguing notion that the distinction between product and process is located in class difference:

> one can distinguish capitalist and working-class theorizations of power on the basis of the specific economic activities each takes as paradigmatic for understanding/explaining power relations. Explanations whose class content Marx would label "bourgeois" tend to privilege activities having to do with money—using it to buy things, investing it in order to increase it, banking it. "Proletarian" explanations take the *activity of production* as the paradigm for power relations. (4; my emphasis)

This is an intriguing suggestion, and one that could serve to explain how Munro's strong desire to become a writer (process) is often at odds with sociocultural ideologies of authorship (product). The field of cultural production puts "serious" writers in an ironic bind; the disavowal of the economic is essential to the maintenance of artistic integrity, as is a disdain for bourgeois values and those who profess them; yet the authors' cultural bankers, their academic canonizers, and even their reading audience, to a large extent, are bourgeois. Munro's difficulty with the disjunction between authorship and writing is further compounded by her own perceived class position.

Furthermore, the subject position of serious artist is inherently risky in both economic and psychological terms. In a 1980 *Globe and Mail* piece titled "To Write, Perchance to Eat," Yves Lavigne addresses the economics of literary authorship, commenting that "a survey by Statistics Canada shows that most writers live below the poverty line. Of an estimated 3,000 writers in this country, maybe fifty could live from their writing" (F7).[1] Lavigne describes the serious Canadian writer as "perched precariously between art and commercialism," and cites Gary Geddes's comment that "If you lean too far one way, you lose your art. If you lean too far the other way, you lose your public." Lavigne remarks that: "Readers today are voracious consumers who want to be entertained, not enlightened, and serious fiction and poetry don't meet their definition of a good read....Take away university professors and their courses, graduate students, writers and critics, and the market for serious Canadian fiction would disappear along with them" (F7). Lavigne then cites William Faulkner's remark that "the writer doesn't want success...he wants to leave a scratch on [the] wall...that somebody a hundred, or a thousand years later will see" (F7). This typical artistic statement reflects Bourdieu's argument that, in the field of restricted production, the belief that "success is suspect and asceticism in this world is the precondition for salvation in the next" is based primarily on "the economy of cultural production itself" (101), in which artistic integrity is founded on its difference from the bourgeois audience that consumes its products. However, according to Bourdieu, "one of the great covert truths underlying the aestheticism of art for art's sake" is this:

> The opposition between art for art's sake and middle-brow art which, on the ideological plane, becomes transformed into an opposition between the idealism of devotion to art and the cynicism of submission to the market, should not hide the fact that the desire to oppose a specifically cultural legitimacy to the prerogatives of power and money constitutes one more way of recognizing that business is business. (*Field* 128)

In other words, the producer's disavowal of the economic, her practice of disinterestedness, is in fact a covert acknowledgement of the power of economics in the cultural field. Part of Munro's sense of fraudulence in the public role of author may attest to her awareness of this fact.

While Munro successfully challenges ideologies of nationality and genre, it is in the identity markers of "woman" and "writer" that, despite her active resistance, she is not so fully empowered. In the case of "writer," class distinctions are certainly important; Munro sees herself as an anomaly in the restricted field, judging that persons of her social class rarely become serious writers. Her anxieties about her lack of flamboyance, her intuitive, rather than intellectual, approach, and her writing process (unfavourably compared with that of other writers) are an instance of her sense of seeking admission to a "select club" to which she really can't belong. Tillie Olsen remarks that for writers from the dominated classes, there is "Little to validate our different sense of reality, to help raise one's own truths, voice, against the prevalent" (264). Bourdieu comments on the relationship between class and position in the cultural field by noting an "an extraordinary correspondence between the hierarchy of positions (e.g. of genres and, within genres, of styles) and the hierarchy of social origins." For example, he observes that the popular novel, "more often than any category of novel, is abandoned to writers issuing from the dominated classes and women's writers" (*Field* 189). In light of this observed correspondence between class and genre, Munro's sense that she is never really secure in her position as a serious writer is easily understood. However, it is also important to bear in mind that the literary field of nineteenth- and twentieth-century France described by Bourdieu is more rigidly class-structured than that of late-twentieth-century Canada. The self-conscious burgeoning of a national literature in this country appears to make room for many writers from less-than-privileged backgrounds, such as Milton Acorn, Al Purdy, Gwendolyn MacEwen—and Alice Munro herself.

Whereas class difference is an important but slippery issue in authorship, the interdependence and mutual exclusiveness of gender and authority are easily identified. Issues of gender certainly bubble to the surface in Lavigne's article. For example, Lavigne remarks that poet Patrick Lane "works hard in a bungalow in Regina while his girlfriend [the award-winning poet Lorna Crozier] works to support him" (F7), and he quotes Canadian popular novelist Richard Rohmer as attributing his success to the fact that, "I don't write about the psychological problems of fat girls in Toronto," a sneering reference, I suspect, to Atwood's *Lady Oracle*.[2] Finally, Lavigne remarks on the vicious circle of writer-in-residence appointments, in which authors "vacate, re-locate, and occasionally, even fornicate. It seems that poets, historically impecunious, are much sought after by over-perfumed matrons in the guise of muses" (F7). Lavigne does not mention whether impecunious women writers are deluged with lustful proposals from martini-scented corporate types in the guise of patrons.

Chris Weedon comments that: "Subjectivity works most efficiently for the established hierarchy of power relations in a society when the subject position, which the individual assumes within a particular discourse, is fully identified by the individual with her interests" (112). This comment follows a discussion of Foucault's *History of Sexuality*, which details the "hysterization" of women's bodies by modern science from the eighteenth century onwards, in which the female body was understood as "saturated with sexuality"; was "integrated" into medical practice by making childbirth and menopause pathological; and was "placed in organic communication with the social body...the family space...and the life of children" (qtd. in Weedon 108). Weedon argues that "This discursive production of the nature of women's bodies was central to the reconstitution of social norms of femininity, the patriarchal subjection of women and their exclusion from most aspects of public life" (109). The gendered nature of individual self-formation is part of Munro's anxiety regarding authorship. Because the ideology of "woman" locates itself not in any external fact, like birthplace, class, or literary genre, but in her very body, then ideologies surrounding womanhood, located as they are *in the body*, are of course "fully identified by the individual with her best interests." Thus, very early on in her career, Munro recognizes that "achievement and ability" are perhaps not in her best interests as a woman; these authorial qualities are things for which she may not be "forgiven." In "Paradoxes and Dilemmas: The Woman as Writer," Margaret Atwood tells a story of an established male writer who says to an up-and-coming young woman: "You may be a good writer, but I wouldn't want to fuck you" (185). The dilemma is clear—literary authority, for a woman, can be costly in terms of her identity and value as a woman.

The ideological tensions implicit in female authority are increasingly evident in the evolving self-construction of Munro's interviews. In her early years, Munro described herself proudly as a "housewife,"[3] telling one interviewer that "writing's something I did, like the ironing" (E1), and another: "If I hadn't been able to afford a washing machine, I would have given up on writing" (Ward D6). In short, the early Munro constructs herself as an ordinary housewife who finds time to write. In a 1990 interview, however, Munro describes her drive to succeed as "a kind of monomania about being a writer" (Rasporich 3). In short, the "ordinariness" of her early days is now seen as pathological, driven, a type of mania. Neither self-construction indicates a large measure of comfort with the role of woman author.

Likewise in 1979, discussing the difficulty of balancing motherhood and authorship, Munro says, "I didn't think of myself as a writer until I was 35....Until then I was somebody who had responsibilites to her children, and found some time to sit at the typewriter. The children came first" (Ward D6). However, in the *Paris Review* interview in 1994, she guiltily confesses, "Some part of me was absent for those children....When my oldest daughter was about two, she'd come to where I was sitting at the typewriter, and I would bat her away with one hand and type with the other....This was bad because it made her the adversary to what was most important to me" (McCulloch and Simpson 254). Munro concludes that when she looks back on her early years, she sees herself as "'a hardhearted young woman.' I'm a far more conventional woman than I was then" (253). Certainly, a part of that conventionalizing may have to do with the wisdom of worldly experience which differentiates one's forties from one's sixties, but I think it also relates very closely to the threat to herself as woman that is posed by her increasing literary stature or authority. In "Paradoxes and Dilemmas," Atwood describes her frustration at being expected to "think two sets of thoughts about the same things, one set as a writer or person, the other as a woman....Thus Woman and Writer are often treated as separate categories; but in any individual woman writer, they are inseparable" (180-81). Munro's changing view of herself as a woman and as a writer reflects how this ideological split gains power as the woman writer's authority grows.

At the outset of this study, I suggested that an ideological gap exists between the theorization of the literary and the actual production and consumption of literary texts. The foregoing chapters have attempted to measure some of the dimensions of that gap, through what Bourdieu terms "the reintroduction of the specialists" (*Field* 181) such as mentor, agent, publisher, and peer. But the non-specialists must not be forgotten, either—namely Munro's readers. Sean Burke observes how, in contemporary theory, the Reader is too often treated as a "hollow subject function" (69); however, these hollow subjects come very much to life in the fan mail collected in Munro's archive. By "reader," I do not mean the critic or student or scholar—the type of reader who consumes text for the specific purpose of drawing what Munro herself describes as "profitable conclusions" about it ("Colonel's Hash" 181). The reader I introduce here is an ordinary consumer of cultural products who purchases or borrows a literary text in search of a less tangible profit—pleasure, perhaps, or escape, or enlightenment.

Unquestionably, the theme that recurs most often in Munro's fan mail is *desire*. Dionne Brand claims that "Writing is an act of desire, as is reading. Why does someone enclose a set of apprehensions within a book? Why does someone else open that book, if not in the act of wanting to be wanted, to be understood, to be seen, to be loved?" (138). Certainly, some fan letters take the form of merely polite praise. One, dated April 1969, reads "As fellow members of the Bank Street PTA, as residents of Victoria and Canadians, we are proud to know that books such as yours are receiving rewarding recognition" (MsC 37.2.55.4), a letter that must have been particularly vindicating for the young "housewife" Munro. Yet desire comes into play subtly even here, for, in their association with and recognition of Munro, the members of the Bank Street PTA are elevated also. Praise is certainly a useful vehicle for the articulation of readerly desire. For example, a female professor of literature writes on 19 August 1967 to thank Munro, saying, "you probably shortened my analysis. (Makes me feel that I owe you a fee)" (Acc. 396/87.3 Box 2 File 6). Another female reader, a visual artist, acknowledges Munro as an inspiration, saying "the fact is some days are just tough but when I think about someone like you who wrote anyway, I know I can paint anyway and I do" (Acc. 396/87.3 Box 2 File 3). A sixteen-year-old female reader writes, after reading "Boys and Girls": "I keep hoping the girl will win out; the ending is a cutting, crushing blow for me. I do not want to be a girl. I still believe that is the rottenest thing that can happen to someone. I inwardly protest it. It is a conflict I am not able to resolve; perhaps you have an answer" (MsC 37.2.55.11).

On the other hand, a mature woman reader remarks on how Munro's work elevates women: "I can see so much of my mother and other women I know well and myself in your stories....You are able to make a woman proud to be a woman just by the sheer beauty of your writing and your basically unique insights" (MsC 37.2.55.13). Another woman reader offers Munro material from her own life for the author's fictional purposes. Having recounted a long, complicated (and not particularly interesting) episode in her daughter's life, this reader comments, "That's not the end of the story, but it's as far as it has gone to date. Maybe you can use it, maybe not. But I thought it might be of interest to you" (Acc. 396/87.3 Box 2 File 6). In some cases, readerly desire extends beyond the work and into the personal, as in this confessional letter from a female reader in the United States in 1975: "I have gotten great pleasure out of finishing a story and then staring at your face. It has come to life and become a friend. The smiling wrinkles and warmth have become familiar to me, and you seem more real....I love you" (MsC 37.2.55.14). These women readers not only offer Munro recognition for her achievements; their letters also betray a desire for self-recognition—as women, as friends, as artists, as storytellers, as those who know what art is.

If female readers sometimes express their recognition in terms of a desire for loving friendship, the approaches of male readers can be more overtly sexual. A male fan writing in 1978 says that he was moved to read Munro's work "When I saw that photograph, of an open face with intelligent eyes and with hair that had not been a recent, at least, recipient of narcissistic attention, and with a glimmer of self-conscious rebelliousness" (MsC 37.2.55.23). This letter is particularly striking for the sexual innuendo in the reader's language such as "savoring every juicy modifier," "lingering over each evocative sentence," and "seduced over the brink." The infatuation of the sixteen-year-old reader from New York, whose letter opens chapter 1 of this book, is also evident. He writes to "find out the truth" of Munro's stories, saying that this is his first letter to a writer or movie star. This young man questions the author on her "real" background, and announces that he is "hooked" on Munro. The letter closes with a disjointed postscript that reads: "I never realized how much I loved my dog until the time came when I had to give it away. I would really like to see your garden....I hope to follow in your footsteps and be one of [sic] future's greats" (MsC 37.2.55.7). The author's photograph produces quite a different response from the reader whose letter is cited at the beginning of this chapter, a man who describes *The Beggar Maid* as "a cesspool of filth" and remarks, "Believe me if I had written such a book I would never in this world have had the nerve to publish my picture on the jacket as you did. I can't imagine any Govenor [sic] giving you any kind of award for such a book" (MsC 38.2.74.3). In all three letters, Munro's female perspective has aroused desire, and has invited these men to recognize and articulate desire (or, in the case of the man in Missouri, his own horror at the contemplation of the fact of desire).

The readers' recognition of Munro's Canadian-ness varies. A young Canadian writer remarks, "Everything in your stories is universal. It is as if your realities are totally displacing my own....Despite your Canadian settings, I have never considered you a Canadian writer" (Acc. 396/87.3 Box 2 File 6). However, the Canadian settings of Munro's stories are what attract another male reader, an international flight attendant. Having discovered one of Munro's books in a hotel lobby in Casablanca, he finds that the stories are "a kind of link with what at this point in time seems like another life" (Acc. 396/87/3 Box 2 File 6). From the other side of the world, a male reader in India writes to advise Munro to use allusions to colonial icons like Shakespeare and Sir

Walter Scott in her next book; he also asks her to send him some books, saying "To illustrate my poverty, I have foregone this days [*sic*] food to post this letter." Incidentally, his aerogram is addressed as follows:

> To Alice Munro
> Famous Novelist & Writer
> Clinton
> Ontorio [*sic*] Canada (Acc. 396/87.3 Box 2 file 6)

The fact that Munro received this missive certainly attests to her "fame."

The fan letter that truly confirmed, for me, Bourdieu's description of the literary field as a "universe of belief" (164) is from a cabinetmaker in the northeastern United States, writing to the author about her uncollected story, "Wood." This reader describes his enthusiastic response to the story, and says "I feel you'll appreciate knowing you reached this reader to that extent" (Acc. 396/87.3 Box 2 File 6). He then concludes with a postscript: "Tell Roy [the central character in the story] the woods here are almost nothing but oak." The fact that this reader asks the author to "tell" a fictional character something indicates the power of the "universe of belief" in which the reader functions. Doubtless, the cabinetmaker *knows* that Roy does not exist; but, paradoxically, he believes in his belief in Roy's existence enough to address him through the author who created him.

Reading these fan letters makes me think of my grandmother, who passed away in 1997, in her eighty-seventh year. For the last decade or so of her life, Grandma became increasingly forgetful and, unfortunately, somewhat delusional. It seemed that every time anything went missing in her apartment, such as keys, a book, some face powder, she blamed the disappearance on a cleaning woman who briefly worked for her long ago, but of whom nothing had been seen or heard for years. In time, as Grandma became more forgetful, she imagined that the cleaning woman's entire family were sneaking into the apartment and hiding the *TV Guide*, throwing clothes on the floor, and even kicking the dog. My family tended to laugh off these delusions.

One day, I made the mistake of joking about these phantoms to our family doctor, an old-fashioned general practitioner who provided kind and compassionate care to my entire family, but especially to my grandmother, for more than thirty years. The doctor did not appreciate my joke; he gave me a severe look and said, "Well, they may not be real to you, but they're real to *her*." In short, the doctor insisted that I accord respect to my grandmother's belief, even while maintaining my own disbelief.

In the same way, respect must be accorded to the way Munro's created world is real to her readers. Bourdieu compares the author to a magician, the "*collective misrecognition*" of the audience being "the source of the power the magician appropriates." Like the magician, the author's performance is:

> a *valid imposture*, a legitimate abuse of power, collectively misrecognized and so recognized. The artist who puts her name on a ready-made article and produces an object whose market price is incommensurate with its cost of production is collectively mandated to perform a magic act which would be nothing without the whole tradition leading up to her gesture, and without the universe of celebrants and believers who give it meaning and value in terms of this tradition. (81)

Munro's work may be a juncture of intentionalities and an ideological struggle, but as far as these readers—these "celebrants and believers"—are concerned, it's real to them.

A large part of the desire I read in Munro's fan mail is the desire to be *recognized*, to be acknowledged, as individuals, as Brand suggests. Munro describes this type of desire aptly in the conclusion of "White Dump": As Isabel is irresistibly drawn into an extramarital affair, she feels "rescued, lifted, beheld, and safe" (*Progress* 421). In the archival fan mail files, Munro's readers express a similar kind of desire—to be rescued, lifted, beheld and safe. Whatever the ideological struggles that underlie the production of a literary text, the readerly desire for recognition of his/her own unique humanity remains constant.

In *The Rules of Art,* Bourdieu insists that "Renouncing the angelic belief in a pure interest in pure form is the price we must pay for understanding those social universes" that participate in the construction of authorship. However, Bourdieu's ultimate aim (and mine) is neither smug, cynical, nor destructive; rather, the task is undertaken in order to "offer a vision more true and, ultimately, more reassuring, because less superhuman, of the highest achievements of the human enterprise" (xx). When I began this project of applying cultural studies research to literary archives, what I expected to find was blatant evidence of the bullying interference of American male power brokers on the literary texts of a struggling Canadian woman writer. What I found instead was an interdependent system of ideologies and power relations far more subtle and complex than I could have imagined, in addition to a writing subject exerting more agency and resistance, in equally complex and subtle ways, than I'd anticipated.

As I have shown, the progress of Munro's authorship is profoundly affected by ideological factors related to nationality, gender, genre, and class. But these issues are not clearcut. The small Canadian market and the limitations of Canadian cultural legitimacy in the international field are played off against the less rigid class/educational biases of late-twentieth-century Canada and the burgeoning of a national literature in Munro's sociohistorical moment. Likewise, Munro's gender works against her in some ways; for example, Robert Lecker notes in *Open Letter* that, even in recent years, only 30-35 percent of the contributors to Canadian anthologies are women (44-46). However, in other ways, such as her place as a "women's" writer in an era of second-wave feminism, literary culture provides a space for her, and gender works to her advantage. In the area of genre, the problems created by the privileging of the novel over the short story are significantly offset by the welcoming market for short fiction in Canada (courtesy of Robert Weaver and the CBC), and by the fortuitous embracing of Munro's work by American cultural institutions like the *New Yorker* and *Best American Short Stories* (*BASS*). Michelle Gadpaille has noted that Canadian short fiction writers have an advantage over writers from other non-American English-speaking cultures, in that Canadians are lumped in with Americans in *BASS* and thus have a greater access to publication there than do "foreign" writers, whose work appears in separate "token" editions (116-17). Finally, the question of the writer's role as it relates particularly to social class and education is complicated by the fact that Munro's own characterization of herself as "lower caste" and non-intellectual contends with her privileged ethnicity (Scots/Irish), race (white), nationality (First World), sexual orientation (heterosexual), and literary style ("realist," mainstream).

One of the difficulties of a cultural studies approach is that it may not provide the type of conclusiveness that readers expect of a scholarly work. For me, however, the fascination, and the utility, of this kind of analysis is not so much the conclusions it reaches as the questions and new reading strategies it suggests. Where cultural studies criticism *can* succeed is in propelling the "disenchantment" of the reader in his/her relationship with the literary text, allowing a reading position in which the reader is not "at the mercy" (to use a Munro phrase) of the literary text and its ideological structures.

Thus, though my study of Munro's authorship may raise more questions than it answers, what I believe I have shown is the immense potential of literary archives, analyzed in conjunction with published literary, scholarly, and popular texts, in identifying the questions that beg to be asked and the complex social relations that must be considered in the asking. In short, I am no longer the same reader who picked up "Initram" and was, inexplicably, vaguely offended by its transgressions. In the process of acquainting myself with the dimensions of the cultural field, I have come to know and recognize the author not as a divinely gifted individual, but rather as an admirably resourceful and determined fellow human being. Even more importantly, I have begun to recognize the expectations, desires, and misrecognitions inherent in my own subject position as a consumer of literary texts. If, in this study, I take the cultural critic's role in making profitable conclusions, I am also mindful of my place as reader, one of the faithful who participate in the consecration and celebration of the author and her art.

## Appendix 1: An Overview of Fair Use

The Canadian Copyright Act permits "fair dealing"—i.e., direct quotations from "limited portions" of a work—for purposes of review and criticism. In both the United States and Canada, the definition of "limited portions" is dependent on a number of factors.

The "fair dealing" provision described in sections 29, 29.1, and 29.2 of the Canadian Copyright Act provides that "it is not an infringement of copyright to deal 'fairly' with work for five named purposes: research, private study, criticism, review and news reporting. For the latter three purposes, the law also requires that the source and the author's name be mentioned."

The American and Canadian statutes are similar, and I cite these examples from the United States as illustrations of how such regulations are applied in court.

In *Unpublished Materials*, LeClercq lists four factors that are taken into consideration in a deliberation on fair use:

1) The purpose and character of the use—including whether the purpose is commercial or non-profit—the assumption being that it is nobler to use the author's "property" with intent to teach rather than to profit.

2) The nature of the copyrighted work. Is it public or private? Again, "public" work, or a version of a work later released to the public, is more likely to be found fairly used than a personal letter.

3) The amount and substantiality of the portion used in relation to the whole, that is, the researcher must "author" his own work, bring forth his own ideas, not just "use" the ideational property of the author.

4) The effect of the use on the potential market for or value of the copyrighted work. Because the author authored it, s/he has the right to realize monetary gain from it.

LeClercq then outlines several cases in which the fair use statute was invoked.

- The memoirs of former president Gerald Ford were purchased by Harper and Row. The prepublication contract included exclusive first serial rights for *Time* magazine to publish an excerpt of up to 7,500 words from the forthcoming book. However, the *Nation* obtained a copy of Ford's manuscript and printed a 2,500-word article, which quoted verbatim about 400 words from the memoir. *Time* then abandoned its plan to publish an article on Ford's memoir, and refused to pay Harper and Row the agreed amount. Harper and Row then sued the *Nation* for copyright violation. The court ruled against the *Nation* because "Usurping an author's prepublication rights (by quoting from an unpublished manuscript) infringes 'the author's right to decide when and whether' a work should be made public" (111).

- In the Salinger case, a biographer attempted to use seventy letters written by J.D. Salinger, which had been deposited by recipients' estates in several university libraries. LeClercq says that, while the *Nation* unlawfully used "a prepublication manuscript with substantial prospect and expectation of earnings" (113), the Salinger biographer had gathered "a dispersed set of letters of whose existence the author was unaware" (113). Salinger lost the first trial, the judge ruling that "he has suffered not from copyright infringement but from the publication of a biography that trespasses on his wish for privacy" (115). In other words, as an author, he has already given up his personal privacy. However, on appeal, the appeals judge decided that fair use was outweighed in this case *not* by the sanctity of authorial privacy but by the proprietary interest of the author in his work, "the author's right to control the first public appearance of his undisseminated expression" (115). LeClercq concludes that, in the Salinger case, while the first court saw the biographer's right to use material "in producing and creating an accurate and vivid new historical account...of primary social importance" (117), the second valorized Salinger's ownership of potentially marketable material.

· The proprietary impulse is clear in a case involving the papers of author Richard Wright. Wright's widow, the copyright owner, had sold the papers to Yale and had agreed to their "use." However, when a biographer "used" these papers in her research, Mrs Wright took her to court for violation of copyright. In the biographer's favour were the fact that she was careful to paraphrase rather than quote, and that she gave straight factual reportage; furthermore, her subject was deceased, so personal privacy was not an issue.

Both courts ruled against Mrs Wright. In this case, the importance to society of increased knowledge overrides the protection of private property. While an author's relatives may legally own material, their rights to it are more limited than those of the author him/herself.

### Appendix 2: Short Story Anthologies Edited by Robert Weaver or John Metcalf

#### Robert Weaver

*Canadian Short Stories* (with Helen James). Toronto: Oxford UP, 1952.

*Canadian Short Stories.* Toronto: Oxford UP, 1960. Rept. 1966.

*Ten for Wednesday Night: A Collection of Short Stories Presented for Broadcast by CBC Wednesday Night.* Toronto: McClelland and Stewart, 1961.

*The First Five Years: A Selection from the* Tamarack Review. Toronto: Oxford UP, 1962.

*Canadian Short Stories.* 2nd Series. Toronto: Oxford UP, 1968.

*The Oxford Anthology of Canadian Literature* (with William Toye). Toronto: Oxford UP, 1973.

*Canadian Short Stories.* 3rd Series. Toronto: Oxford UP, 1978.

*The Oxford Anthology of Canadian Literature* (with William Toye). 2nd ed. Toronto: Oxford UP, 1981.

*Small Wonders: New Stories by Twelve Distinguished Canadian Authors.* Toronto: CBC, 1982.

*The* Anthology *Anthology: A Selection from 30 Years of CBC Radio's* Anthology. Toronto: Macmillan, 1984.

*Canadian Short Stories* 4th Series. Toronto: Oxford UP, 1985.

*The Oxford Book of Canadian Short Stories* (with Margaret Atwood). Toronto: Oxford UP, 1986.

*Canadian Short Stories.* 5th Series. Toronto: Oxford UP, 1991.

*The New Oxford Book of Canadian Short Stories* (with Margaret Atwood). Toronto: Oxford UP, 1995.

*Emergent Voices: CBC Literary Awards Stories, 1979-1999.* Fredricton, NB: Goose Lane, 1999.

**John Metcalf**

*Sixteen by Twelve: Short Stories by Canadian Writers.* Toronto: McGraw-Hill Ryerson, 1970.

*The Narrative Voice: Short Stories and Reflections by Canadian Authors.* Toronto: McGraw-Hill Ryerson, 1972.

*Best Canadian Stories 1976.* Ottawa: Oberon P, 1976.

*Best Canadian Stories 1977.* Ottawa: Oberon P, 1977.

*Here and Now: Canadian Stories* (with Clark Blaise). Ottawa: Oberon P, 1977.

*Best Canadian Stories 1978* (with Clark Blaise). Ottawa: Oberon P, 1978.

*Best Canadian Stories 1979* (with Clark Blaise). Ottawa: Oberon P, 1979.

*Stories Plus: Canadian Stories with Authors' Commentaries.* Toronto: McGraw-Hill Ryerson, 1979.

*Best Canadian Stories 1980* (with Clark Blaise). Ottawa: Oberon P, 1980.

*First Impressions.* Ottawa: Oberon P, 1980.

*New Worlds: A Canadian Collection of Stories with Notes.* Toronto: McGraw-Hill Ryerson, 1980.

*Best Canadian Stories 1981* (with Leon Rooke). Ottawa: Oberon P, 1981.

*Second Impressions.* Ottawa: Oberon P, 1981.

*Best Canadian Stories 1982* (with Leon Rooke). Ottawa: Oberon P, 1982.

*Kaleidoscope: Canadian Stories.* Scarborough, ON: Nelson, 1982.

*Making It New: Contemporary Canadian Stories.* Toronto: Methuen, 1982.

*Third Impressions.* Ottawa: Oberon P, 1982.

*The New Press Anthology* (with Leon Rooke). Toronto: General Publishing, 1984.

*The New Press Anthology* (with Leon Rooke). Toronto: General Publishing, 1985.

*The Macmillan Anthology 1* (with Leon Rooke). Toronto: Mac-millan, 1988.

*The Macmillan Anthology 2* (with Leon Rooke). Toronto: Macmillan, 1989.

*The Macmillan Anthology 3* (with Kent Thompson). Toronto: Macmillan, 1990.

*The New Story Writers.* Kingston, ON: Quarry Press, 1992.

*Canadian Classics: An Anthology of Short Stories.* Toronto: McGraw-Hill Ryerson, 1993.

*How Stories Mean.* Erin, ON: Porcupine's Quill, 1993.

# NOTES

## CHAPTER I

1 For a detailed discussion of the relationship between Munro and "Initram," see chapter 5.

2 The term "generic contract" comes from Timothy Dow Adams, *Telling Lies in Modern American Autobiography*, p. 12.

3 For a more detailed discussion of fair use, see Appendix 1.

4 For example, the 1998 Giller Prize for *The Love of a Good Woman* and months atop the bestseller lists in Canada and abroad.

5 Excerpts from reviews on the back cover of *Open Secrets*, 1994.

6 The basis for this identification is the many samples of Munro's handwriting available in the archive. Many of her first-draft manuscripts are handwritten in coil notebooks, and several notebooks contain similar cartoon drawings as well.

7 Many files in the archive are closed to researchers, and copies of Munro's personal correspondence are not included in her archive. Many "restricted" files, as far as I can determine from the catalogue entries describing these items, are related to financial information.

8 In Richler's *Joshua Then and Now*, the central character gleefully sells his papers to "Rocky Mountain U," including a concocted correspondence meant to trick some drudging graduate student into believing that a homosexual relationship existed between Joshua and another literary figure. Richler's papers were purchased by the University of Calgary in 1974. A.S. Byatt's *Possession: A Romance* and Carol Shields's *Swann: A Literary Mystery* examine the greedy possessiveness and ambition of academic researchers. David

Lodge's comic novels of academic life, such as *Small World,*
*Changing Places,* and *Nice Work,* all lampoon many aspects of literary scholarship.

9  From Adrienne Rich's *On Lies, Secrets and Silence* (New York:
   Norton, 1979).

10 Letter from Virginia Barber to Robert Thacker, Nov. 11, 1998.

11 See chapter 5 for a detailed discussion of this essay.

## CHAPTER II

1  See appendix 2 for a list of anthologies edited by Weaver.

2  This and the three preceding quotations are from a tribute entitled
   "Bob Weaver Has Lots of Friends."

3  See Stewart, 155, for this "variation" on the theme: "when Kildare
   Dobbs sold a poem to *Anthology,* nobody heard it, because Bob
   Weaver was having a party that night and all of the *Anthology* lis-
   teners were at Weaver's house."

4  See page 37 of this chapter and note 6 below.

5  According to the Canada Council Access to Information Service,
   Munro has received only one writer's grant from the Canada
   Council, a Senior Arts Grant in the amount of $7500, in 1972-73.

6  Smith's assertion was brought home to me when I taught a senior-
   level seminar in a survey course of Canadian literature at the
   University of Calgary in 1994. I began our seminar by asking my
   students to name their favourite Canadian author. Silence reigned.
   I then asked them to name any Canadian author. "Farley Mowat?"
   somebody guessed.

7  Gzowski's question is: "What are some of your favourite stories?
   Who do you read, what short story writers do you read?" Munro
   responds: "Well, I'll say right at the beginning that I'm not going to
   mention any Canadians, not because I don't read Canadian short
   stories but because I'm so afraid I will leave someone out whom I
   greatly admire." This reticence is a relatively recent development.
   As late as 1987, Munro freely names her favourite Canadian writers
   in interviews, for example, Hancock, p. 204. Perhaps her present
   reluctance to name names is a function of her increased power and
   authority, and/or a function of the increased power and authority
   of what Russell Smith describes as the "Canon crows."

8  A comparison of the novels released by these three foremost
   Canadian woman writers in the early 1970s makes the point. They
   are Munro's *Lives of Girls and Women* (1972), Atwood's *Surfacing*
   (1972), and Laurence's *The Diviners* (1974).

   *The Diviners,* which Laurence describes as her "spiritual autobiography," explores personal and cultural identity through the char-

acter of Morag Gunn, woman writer, whose movements away from and within Canada are part of a search for a mythic and actual "home." Desperate to escape the parochialism of small-town Manitoba, Morag embraces the colonial patriarch Brooke Skelton. A professor of English literature, Skelton, whom Morag marries, is both repressed and repressive, a product of colonial India, a sexual and intellectual patriarch. Morag ultimately rejects Brooke in favour of the native/Native tradition personified by the Metis musician and storyteller Jules Tonnerre. Her choice allows both sexual and personal liberation (fertility and self-reliance) and artistic/intellectual freedom.

Atwood's *Surfacing* appeared in the same year as *Survival*, her critical work on themes in Canadian literature, and indeed, the unnamed narrator of the novel acts out many of Atwood's theories of victimization and the struggle for psychic/emotional survival. The narrator of *Surfacing* is engaged in a search for her father, her history, her primal self. The enemy, or spectre, in this text, however, is not the colonial British tradition, but the near and present threat of psychic/economic/cultural engulfment by rapacious and greedy "Americans." W.H. New describes *Surfacing* as "expressive of the radical nationalism which characterized much Canadian life in the early 70's" (273). As in *The Diviners*, the central character of *Surfacing* ultimately seeks Native culture as a guide to returning to nature, to retrieving her fundamental selfhood.

While Munro's *Lives of Girls and Women* resembles the other two novels in its entwining of the sexual with the artistic/intellectual search for self-definition, the novel is profoundly regional; the focus is not on national identity but on the town of Jubilee, with its secrets, its grotesqueries, its "deep caves paved with kitchen linoleum" (210). It is the particularity of the town itself that engages Del Jordan, and she envisions her salvation in the understanding and rendering of these particularities. She makes lists of every detail of town history, but "no list could hold what I wanted, for what I wanted was every last thing, every layer of speech and thought, stroke of light on bark or walls, every smell, pothole, pain, crack, delusion, held still and held together—radiant, everlasting" (210).

9  In a letter dated 24 January 1956, held in the Robert Weaver Collection at the National Archives of Canada, Weaver congratulates Munro on recent publications in *Queen's Quarterly* and *Chatelaine*, then goes on to say: "I wonder if you have tried to send any fiction to the United States? I have often thought that you might find it useful and interesting to have some comments from editors in the United States, and I am sure that some of the more

serious magazines there would at least be interested in reading some of your stories."

10  Munro placed three stories in *McCall's* in the seventies: "Red Dress-1946" in March 1973, "How I Met My Husband" in February 1974, and "Forgiveness in Families" in April 1974.

11  However, since that period, her output has been very regular: *Who Do You Think You Are?* (1978), *The Moons of Jupiter* (1982), *The Progress of Love* (1986), *Friend of My Youth* (1990), *Open Secrets* (1994), and *The Love of a Good Woman* (1998). An edition of *Selected Stories* appeared in the fall of 1996, but this text contained no previously unpublished work. However, the collection *Hateship, Friendship, Courtship, Loveship, Marriage* (Fall 2001) appeared only three years after the previous book.

12  A holograph notation in the author's hand is my source for this assertion.

13  On 18 May 1951, Weaver rejects a Munro story called "The Widower," saying "you have rather failed to rise above somewhat commonplace and tedious material." On 3 October 1952, he describes the situation depicted in "The Man from Melbury" as "a trifle commonplace" and the violent ending "a trifle convenient and contrived." In the same letter, Weaver also rejects "The Shivaree," finding it "almost tedious" and noting that "most readers would finally react not with sympathy but with a rather strong feeling of simple discomfort." A letter of 24 January 1956 describes how "Thanks for the Ride" creates in Weaver "some doubt whether it succeeds in being a unified and entirely successful piece of fiction." Finally, on 16 May 1957, Weaver returns "The Cousins," because "I am sorry to say that all of us agree that it isn't a very successful story." All above citations are taken from the Robert Weaver Papers at the National Archives of Canada: MG 31–D162 (18-15C-27).

14  Years, titles, wins and nominations, and juries for the Governor General's Awards to Munro texts are as follows:

| 1968 | *Dance of the Happy Shades* | Award | Robert Weaver (chair)<br>Henry Kreisel<br>Philip Stratford |
| --- | --- | --- | --- |
| 1978 | *Who Do You Think You Are?* | Award | Margaret Laurence (chair)<br>Patrick O'Flaherty<br>Sheila Watson |
| 1982 | *The Moons of Jupiter* | Nominee | W.D. Valgardson (chair)<br>Ronald Sutherland<br>Adele Wiseman |
| 1986 | *The Progress of Love* | Award | Helen Weinzweig (chair)<br>Norman Levine<br>Rudy Wiebe |

| 1990 | *Friend of My Youth* | Nominee | Leon Rooke (chair) |
|      |                      |         | Sandra Birdsell |
|      |                      |         | Henry Kreisel |
| 1994 | *Open Secrets*       | Nominee | M.T. Kelly (chair) |
|      |                      |         | Elisabeth Harvor |
|      |                      |         | Robert Kroetsch |

Source: Canada Council Access to Information Service.

15 *The Beggar Maid* was the title given to *Who Do You Think You Are?* in the United States and Britain.

16 Materials from the Third Accession of the Munro papers are not yet fully catalogued. Thus, when referring to such materials, I cite the temporary number assigned to the accession, as well as a box and file number.

## CHAPTER III

1 I have not been granted permission to quote from Barber's correspondence with Munro for this book; thus, my discussion relies on a summary of my research in this area. For more detailed discussion of the Barber correspondence, as well as excerpts quoted with permission, refer to my article "Alice Munro's Agency: The Virginia Barber Correspondence, 1976-83," *Essays on Canadian Writing* 66 (Winter 1998): 81-102.

2 In an archival clipping titled "The Causerie," Christopher Dafoe refers to a Globe and Mail article, written shortly after Munro's first Governor General's Award, which described her as a "shy housewife." I have been unable to trace original citations for either of these articles, but the hard copy of the clipping is in MsC. 37.20.22. Note also that in her letter of introduction, Barber also describes Munro as "shy" (MsC 37.2.47.2).

3 I assign this undated fragment a date between spring 1976 and spring 1978 [i.e., during the years leading up to the publication of *Who Do You Think You Are?*] based on the fact that 1) Barber refers to Engel's *Bear*, published April 1976, and 2) Barber signs off with the words "Best Wishes." By June 1978, she generally signs her letters "Love, Ginger."

## CHAPTER IV

1 See, for example, Wachtel, *Writers and Company*, CBC Radio, September 1991.

2 Including Raymond Knister, ed., *Canadian Short Stories* (Toronto: Macmillan, 1928); Desmond Pacey, ed., *Book of Canadian Stories* (Toronto: Ryerson, 1947); Robert Weaver and Helen James, eds., *Canadian Short Stories* (Toronto: Oxford University Press, 1952).

3  Five subsequent editions of this anthology have appeared since 1960, the most recent co-edited with Margaret Atwood.

4  The document, reproduced from a 1928 edition of *Best American Stories*, is also interesting for the way in which editor Edward J. O'Brien further categorizes the "distinctiveness" of the stories with a system of asterisks. Three-asterisk stories are judged by O'Brien to be "worth reprinting in book form" (Levy 39). For example, of the 334 *Saturday Evening Post* selections, only 2 per cent are "distinctive" enough to get three asterisks, while 64 percent of the 33 stories that appeared in *Harper's* achieved that level of distinction.

5  For a fascinating discussion of such "contamination" from a contemporary perspective, see Carole L. Beran, "The Luxury of Excellence: Alice Munro in the *New Yorker*," *Essays on Canadian Writing* 66 (Winter 1998): *Alice Munro: Writing On.*

6  Munro's children were born in 1953, 1957, and 1966. In 1955 she gave birth to a daughter who lived only two days.

7  This is true not only of North America; in "A Neglected Responsibility: Contemporary Literary Manuscripts," Philip Larkin deplores the fact that reams of English literary papers are being purchased by American academies. In answer to the question of how archivists are to know which writer's archival materials should be considered valuable, Larkin responds: "Simple. We ask our English departments." See *Encounter* (July 1979): 33-41.

8  The thorny relationship between the writer and the academy is explored in detail in chapter 5, "Writer."

9  The fourth letter, dated 21 August 1978, encloses a rewritten version of "Simon's Luck" (MsC 38.2.64.8a).

10 In her study of an alternate manuscript for this book, Helen Hoy makes extensive use of the University of Calgary archival materials. She remarks that other correspondence between Barber and Munro is held by the Barber agency and is currently closed to researchers. Hoy expresses her hope, echoed by me, that these letters "will become part of the Munro collection sometimes in the future"(p. 80, n. 14). This has not yet occurred. The recent Third Accession does contain 85 items of correspondence from the Barber Agency, but none dated prior to 1981.

11 Hoy p. 82, n. 50 Alice Munro file, W.W. Norton.

12 As mentioned, the character of "Janet" appears in the first, second, and final stories of *The Moons of Jupiter*, while the remaining stories all present different and unrelated characters. None of Munro's subsequent texts have been described, by herself or by critics, as a "novel" or "story sequence."

## CHAPTER V

1 As mentioned in the preface, I have not obtained permission to quote from Munro's letters to Metcalf and thus present her side of the dialogue in summary form.

2 From the Robert Weaver Collection, National Archives of Canada: 24 January 1956 (18-15C-27).

3 Foucault begins his essay "What Is an Author?" by citing Beckett's question: "What does it matter who is speaking?"

4 For analysis of these techniques, see, for example, Ajay Heble, *The Tumble of Reason: Alice Munro's Discourse of Absence* (Toronto: U of Toronto P, 1994); Lorraine McMullen, "'Shameless, Marvellous, Shattering Absurdity': The Humour of Paradox in Alice Munro," *Probable Fictions,* ed. MacKendrick, 144-62; Helen Hoy, "'Dull, Simple, Amazing, Unfathomable': Paradox and Double Vision in Alice Munro's Fiction," *Studies in Canadian Literature* 5 (Spring 1980): 100-15.

5 *Lives of Girls and Women* begins with this disclaimer: "This novel is autobiographical in form if not in fact. My family, neighbours and friends did not serve as models.—A.M." Even at this early point in her career, Munro's "nose" for the field allowed her to see the necessity for this kind of statement.

6 For example, the religious zeal of the mother, Marietta, in "The Progress of Love" is regarded with bewilderment by the narrator. In "Circle of Prayer" the narrator's friend confesses, with some embarrassment, to participating in group prayer. Just prior to this confession, the narrator "had the feeling, from Janet's tone, that she was going to tell her something serious and unpleasant" (365), yet when Trudy hears the word "prayer," she is tempted to laugh aloud. Del Jordan's spiritual quests in "Age of Faith" lead to the conclusion that prayer is useless—"It's not going to do any good. It won't work, it doesn't work"(96). Later stories offer various characters whose religious beliefs mark them as victims at best, such as the retired minister who commits suicide in "Pictures of the Ice," or as amoral hypocrites hiding behind a mask of sanctity, such as the young couple in "Vandals."

7 A trip to China in 1981 with six other writers, as guests of the China Writers' Association (C. Ross 84).

8 The Munro papers contain letters from the University of Toronto offering writer-in-residence positions for the years 1978/79 (MsC 37.2.44) and 1979/80 (MsC 38.2.56.1) in addition to the letter just cited.

## CHAPTER VI

1 The situation is not much better in the United States, which, though it has ten times the population, appears to support only twice as many writers. Tillie Olsen cites a 1976 article in *Poets and Writers Newsletter* that "estimates that there are only a hundred or so writers in this country [the United States] who can actually make a living from their books" (167).

2 The difference between the public reactions to "shy" and "modest" Alice Munro and outspoken activist Margaret Atwood, though outside the scope of this study, is certainly intriguing. It is likely that Munro's reticence serves, among other things, to protect her from the venomous attacks, insulting satires, and misogynistic and antifeminist hostility frequently directed at Atwood.

3 Christopher Dafoe describes having cocktails with the Munros shortly after the publication of *Dance of the Happy Shades*. He says, "At one point, while I was shooting my mouth off about literary methods, I made some scornful remarks about housewives. 'I'm a housewife,' said Mrs. Munro, giving me a mild look" (29A).

# WORKS CITED

## Archival

Alice Munro Papers. Special Collections. University of Calgary Library. Acc. 396/87.3.

John Metcalf Papers. Special Collections. University of Calgary Library. Acc. 559/94, 565/95.3.

Robert Weaver Papers. National Archives of Canada, Ottawa. Acc. MG31D162.

## Published

Adachi, Ken. "Turn Off the TV and Read a Story!" *Toronto Star* 4 Nov. 1978: D7.

Adams, Timothy Dow. *Telling Lies in Modern American Autobiography.* Chapel Hill, NC: U of North Carolina P, 1990.

Althusser, Louis. from "Ideology and Ideological State Apparatuses." *Ideology.* Ed. David Hawke. London: Routledge, 1996. 50-58.

Altick, Richard. *The Scholar Adventurers.* New York: Macmillan, 1951.

Ashcroft, Bill, Gareth Griffiths, and Helen Tiffin. *The Empire Writes Back: Theory and Practice in Post-Colonial Literatures.* London: Routledge, 1989.

Atwood, Margaret. "Paradoxes and Dilemmas: The Woman as Writer." *Woman as Writer.* Ed. Jeannette L. Webber and Joan Grumman. Boston: Houghton Mifflin, 1978. 178-87.

_____. Rev. of *Great Canadian Short Stories,* ed. Alec Lucas in *World Literature Written in English* 11.1 (April 1972): 63-64.

_____. "Sexual Bias in Reviewing." *In the Feminine: Women and Words.* Ed. Ann Dybikowski et al. Edmonton: Longspoon P, 1985. 151-52.

Bader, A.L. "The Structure of the Modern Short Story." May 107-15.

Banting, Pamela. "The Archive as a Literary Genre: Some Theoretical Speculations." *Archivaria* 23 (Winter 1986-7): 119-22.

Barthes, Roland. "The Death of the Author." Burke 125-30.

_____. "The Writer on Holiday." *Mythologies.* London: Paladin, 1973. 31-34.

Belsey, Catherine. *Critical Practice.* London: Routledge, 1991.

Bennett, Donna, and Russell Brown, eds. *An Anthology of Canadian Literature in English.* Vol 2. Toronto: Oxford UP, 1983.

_____. "Conflicted Vision: A Consideration of Canon and Genre in English-Canadian Literature." Lecker *Canadian Canons* 131-49.

Biriotti, Maurice, and Nicola Miller, eds. *What Is an Author?* New York: Manchester UP, 1993.

Bissell, Claude. "Politics and Literature in the 1960's." Klinck, *Literary History of Canada.* Vol. 3. 3-15.

Blaise, Clark. "Mentors." *Canadian Literature* 101 (Summer 1984): 35-41.

"Bob Weaver Has Lots of Friends." *Performing Arts Magazine* (Fall 1973): 13-14.

Bourdieu, Pierre. *The Field of Cultural Production.* London: Columbia UP, 1993.

_____. *The Rules of Art: Genesis and Structure of the Literary Field.* Trans. Susan Emanuel. Stanford: Stanford UP, 1995.

Brand, Dionne. "Arriving at Desire." *Desire in Seven Voices.* Ed. Lorna Crozier. Vancouver: Douglas and McIntyre, 1999. 125-42.

Brothman, Brien. "Orders of Value: Probing the Theoretical Terms of Archival Practice." *Archivaria* 32 (Summer 1991): 78-100.

Buffie, Erna S. "The Massey Report and the Intellectuals: Tory Cultural Nationalism in Ontario in the 1950s." Thesis. U of Manitoba, 1982.

Burke, Sean, ed. *Authorship: From Plato to Postmodern.* Edinburgh: Edinburgh UP, 1995.

_____. "Changing Conceptions of Authorship." *Authorship.* 5-11.

_____. "Introduction: Reconstructing the Author." *Authorship.* xv-xxx.

_____. Introduction to "The Twentieth Century Controversy." *Authorship.* 65-71.

_____. Introduction to "Ideologies and Authorship." *Authorship.* 215-221.

Buss, Helen. *Mapping Ourselves.* Montreal and Kingston: McGill-Queens UP, 1993.

_____. "Reading and Writing Autobiographically." *Prairie Fire* 16.3 (Autumn 1996): 5-15.

Butala, Sharon. "A Walk on the Wild Side with Alice Munro." *Globe and Mail* 17 Sept. 1994: C16.

Byatt, A.S. *Possession: A Romance.* London: Vintage, 1990.

Carrington, Ildiko de Papp. *Alice Munro and Her Works.* Toronto: ECW Press, n.d.

———. *Controlling the Uncontrollable: The Fiction of Alice Munro.* Dekalb, IL: Illinois UP, 1989.

———. *Margaret Atwood and Her Works.* Toronto: ECW Press, 1985.

Chodorow, Nancy. "Family Structure and Feminine Personality." *Women, Culture and Society.* Ed. Michelle Zimbalist Rosaldo and Louise Lamphere. Stanford: Stanford UP, 1974. 43-66.

Chute, Beatrice Henrietta. "Governor General's Canadian Fiction Awards— 1936–1950." Thesis. Acadia U, 1952.

Coles, Don. "Victor Hugo, Alas!" *Globe and Mail* 7 Mar. 1998: D10.

Cooley, Martha. *The Archivist.* Boston: Back Bay Books, 1999.

Crean, S.M. *Who's Afraid of Canadian Culture?* Don Mills, ON: General, 1976.

Dafoe, Christopher. "Books and Bookmen." *Vancouver Sun* 2 May 1969: 29A.

Dahlie, Hallvard. Introduction. Steele 1-5.

Davey, Frank. *From There to Here: A Guide to English-Canadian Literature since 1960.* Erin, ON: Press Porcépic, 1974.

———. *Reading Canadian Reading.* Winnipeg: Turnstone P, 1988.

———. "Genre Subversion in the English-Canadian Short Story."*Reading Canadian Reading.* 137-50.

———. "Writers and Publishers in English-Canadian Literature." *Reading Canadian Reading.* 87-104.

Davis, Lennard J. *Resisting Novels: Ideology and Fiction.* New York: Methuen, 1987.

Docherty, Thomas. "Authority, History and the Question of Postmodernism." Biriotti 53-71.

Drainie, Bronwyn. *Living the Part: John Drainie and the Dilemma of Canadian Stardom.* Toronto: Macmillan, 1988.

During, Simon, ed. Introduction. *The Cultural Studies Reader.* New York: Routledge, 1993. 1-25.

Eagleton, Mary. "Gender and Genre." Hanson 55-68.

Eastwood, Terry. "Nailing a Little Jelly to the Wall of Archival Studies." *Archivaria* 35 (Spring 1993): 232-52.

Faulkner, William. "The *Paris Review* Interview." *Writers at Work.* Ed. Malcolm Cowley. New York: Viking P, 1958. 119-42.

Foucault, Michel. "The Functions of Literature." *Foucault: Politics, Philosophy, Culture.* Ed. Lawrence D. Kritzman. New York: Routledge, 1988. 306-13.

———. "Two Lectures." *Power/Knowledge: Selected Interviews and Other Writings.* New York: Pantheon, 1980. 78-108.

_____. "What Is an Author?" *Contemporary Literary Criticism*. Ed. Robert Con Davis and Ronald Schleifer. New York: Longman, 1989. 262-75.

Gadpaille, Michelle. *The Canadian Short Story*. Toronto: Oxford UP, 1988.

Gallant, Mavis. "Things Overlooked Before." Preface to *The Affair of Gabrielle Russier*. New York: Knopf, 1971.

Gasparini, Len. "Canadian Short Stories." *Globe and Mail* 31 March 1979: C5.

Gilbert, Sandra M., and Susan Gubar. *The Madwoman in the Attic: The Woman Writer and the Nineteenth-Century Literary Imagination*. New Haven, CT: Yale UP, 1979.

Gullason, Thomas A. "The Short Story: An Underrated Art." May 13-31.

Gzowski, Peter. Interview with Alice Munro. *Morningside*. CBC Radio. Oct. 1994

_____. Interview with Alice Munro. *Morningside*. CBC Radio. Oct. 1996.

Hancock, Geoff. "Alice Munro." *Canadian Writers at Work: Interviews with Geoff Hancock*. Toronto: Oxford UP, 1987. 187-224.

Hanson, Clare, ed. *Re-Reading the Short Story*. New York: St Martin's P, 1989. 1-9.

Harker, Richard, Cheleen Mahar, and Chris Wilkes. *An Introduction to the Work of Pierre Bourdieu: The Practice of Theory*. New York: St Martin's P, 1990.

Hartsock, Nancy. *Money, Sex and Power: Toward a Feminist Historical Materialism*. Boston: Northeastern UP, 1983.

Harvey, Sarah. "Short Story Writing That's Long on Talent." *Globe and Mail* 18 March 1995: C7.

Hoy, Helen. "Rose and Janet: Alice Munro's Metafiction." *Canadian Literature* 121 (Summer 1989): 59-84.

Jenkinson, Hilary. "Reflections of an Archivist." *A Modern Archives Reader: Basic Readings in Archival Theory and Practice*. Ed. Maygene F. Daniels and Timothy Walch. Washington: National Archives and Records Service, U.S. General Services Administration, 1984. 15-22.

Johnson, Randal. "Editor's Introduction: Pierre Bourdieu on Art, Literature, and Culture." Bourdieu, *The Field of Cultural Production*. 1-25.

Keefer, Janice Kulyk. "Gender, Language, Genre." *Language in Her Eye*. Ed. Libby Scheier, Sarah Sheard, and Eleanor Wachtel. Toronto: Coach House, 1990. 164-71.

King, Sarah. "The Failure of Canadian Literature." *Open Letter* 9.1 (Fall 1994): 5-24.

Klinck, Carl F., ed. *Literary History of Canada: Canadian Literature in English*. 2nd ed. Vol. 2. Toronto: U of Toronto P, 1976.

_____. *Literary History of Canada: Canadian Literature in English.* 2nd ed. Vol. 3. Toronto: U of Toronto P, 1976.

Knelman, Martin. "The Past, the Present, and Alice Munro." *Saturday Night.* Nov. 1979: 16-22.

Lavigne, Yves. "To Write, Perchance to Eat." *Globe and Mail* 11 Oct. 1980: F7.

Lecker, Robert. "Anthologizing English-Canadian Fiction: Some Canonical Trends." *Open Letter* 9.1 (Fall 1994): 25-80.

_____. ed. *Canadian Canons: Essays in Literary Value.* Toronto: U of Toronto P, 1991.

LeClercq, Angie Whaley. *Unpublished Materials: Libraries and Fair Use.* Washington: Association of Research Libraries, 1993.

Levy, Andrew. *The Culture and Commerce of the American Short Story.* New York: Cambridge UP, 1993.

Lodge, David. *Changing Places.* London: Secker and Warburg, 1975.

_____. *Nice Work.* London: Secker and Warburg, 1988.

_____. *Small World.* London: Secker and Warburg, 1984.

Macherey, Pierre. *A Theory of Literary Production.* Trans. Geoffrey Wall. London: Routledge, 1989.

MacKendrick, Louis K., ed. *Probable Fictions: Alice Munro's Narrative Acts.* Downsview, ON: ECW Press, 1983.

Marchalonis, Shirley. Introduction. *Patrons and Protegees: Gender, Friendship and Writing in Nineteenth-Century America.* New Brunswick, NJ: Rutgers UP, 1988. xi-xviii.

"Margaret Laurence, 1926-1987." *Books in Canada* Jan./Feb. 1987: 3.

Mathews, Lawrence. "Calgary, Canonization, and Class: Deciphering List B." Lecker, *Canadian Canons* 150-68.

Matthews, Brander. "The Philosophy of the Short Story." May 52-59.

May, Charles E., ed. *Short Story Theories.* Athens: Ohio UP, 1976.

McCulloch, Jeanne, and Mona Simpson. "Alice Munro: The Art of Fiction CXXXVII." *Paris Review* 131 (Summer 1994): 227-64.

McPherson, Hugo. "Fiction (1940-1960)." Klinck, *Literary History of Canada* Vol 2. 205-33.

Meese, Elizabeth. "Archival Materials: The Problem of Literary Reputation." *Women in Print I.* Ed. Joan E. Hartman and Ellen Messer-Davidow. New York: MLA, 1982. 37-46.

Metcalf, John, ed. *New Worlds: A Canadian Collection of Stories with Notes.* Toronto: McGraw-Hill Ryerson, 1980.

Moravia, Alberto. "The Short Story and the Novel." May 147-52.

Morley, Patricia. *Margaret Laurence: The Long Journey Home.* Montreal and Kingston: McGill-Queen's UP, 1991.

Munro, Alice. "Author's Commentary." *Sixteen by Twelve: Short Stories by Canadian Writers.* Ed. John Metcalf. Toronto: Ryerson, 1970. 125-26.

_____. "The Beggar Maid." *Who Do You Think You Are?* 67-99.

_____. "A Better Place Than Home." *The Newcomers.* Toronto: McClelland and Stewart, 1979. 113-24.

_____. "The Colonel's Hash Resettled." *The Narrative Voice: Short Stories and Reflections by Canadian Authors.* Ed. John Metcalf. Toronto: McGraw-Hill Ryerson, 1972. 181-83.

_____. *Dance of the Happy Shades.* Toronto: Ryerson, 1968.

_____. Foreword. Weaver, *Anthology.* ix-x.

_____. *Friend of My Youth.* Toronto: Penguin, 1991.

_____. "Home." *New Canadian Stories 74.* Ed. David Helwig and Joan Harcourt. Ottawa: Oberon, 1974. 133-53.

_____. *Lives of Girls and Women.* New York: Signet, 1974.

_____. "Material." *Something I've Been Meaning to Tell You.* 20-36.

_____. *The Moons of Jupiter.* Toronto: McClelland and Stewart, 1982.

_____. *Open Secrets.* Toronto: McClelland and Stewart, 1994.

_____. *The Progress of Love.* Markham, ON: Penguin, 1987.

_____. "Remember Roger Mortimer." *Montrealer* Feb. 1962: 34-37.

_____. "Rich as Stink." *The Love of a Good Woman.* Toronto: McClelland and Stewart, 1998. 215-53.

_____. *Selected Stories.* Toronto: McClelland and Stewart, 1996.

_____. *Something I've Been Meaning to Tell You.* New York: Signet, 1975.

_____. "What Is Real?" *Making It New: Contemporary Canadian Stories.* Ed. John Metcalf. Toronto: Methuen, 1982. 223-26.

_____. *Who Do You Think You Are?* Scarborough, ON: Signet, 1979.

_____. "Working for a Living." *Grand Street* 1.1 (Autumn 1981): 9-37.

Nesbit, Molly. "What Was an Author?" Burke 247-62.

New, W.H. "Fiction." *Literary History of Canada.* Vol. 3. 233-83.

Olsen, Tillie. *Silences.* New York: Delacorte, 1978.

Pacey, Desmond. "Modern Canadian Fiction, 1920-1950." *Creative Writing in Canada.* 2nd. ed. Toronto: Ryerson, 1961. 186-229.

_____. "The Writer and His Public (1920-1960)." Klinck, *Literary History.* Vol. 2. 3-21.

Poe, Edgar Allen. "Review of *Twice-Told Tales.*" May 45-51.

Polk, James. "Deep Caves and Kitchen Linoleum." *Canadian Literature* 54 (Autumn 1972): 102-104.

Rasporich, Beverly. *Dance of the Sexes: Art and Gender in the Fiction of Alice Munro.* Edmonton: U of Alberta P, 1990.

Richler, Mordecai. *Joshua Then and Now.* Toronto: McClelland and Stewart, 1989.

Richler, Noah. "A Generation of Copycats." *National Post* 3 April 2001: B1, 5.

Rosenberg, Jerome H. *Margaret Atwood.* Boston: Twayne, 1984.

Ross, Catherine Sheldrick. *Alice Munro: A Double Life*. Toronto: ECW Press, 1992.

Ross, Oakland. Rev. of *Strangers Are Like Children* by Joan Baxter. *Globe and Mail* 10 Aug. 1996: C8.

Ross, Val. "Weaving a Literary Legacy." *Globe and Mail* 27 Apr. 1994: A9-10.

Scott, F.R. "The Canadian Authors Meet." *Literature in Canada*. Ed. Douglas Daymond and Leslie Monkman. Vol 2. Toronto: Gage, 1978. 98-99.

Scott, Gail. "Shaping a Vehicle for Her Use: Women and the Short Story." *In the Feminine: Women and Words*. Ed. Ann Dybikowski et al. Edmonton: Longspoon P, 1985. 184-91.

Shields, Carol. *Swann: A Literary Mystery*. Toronto: General, 1987.

Slopen, Beverley. "PW Interviews Alice Munro." *Publishers Weekly*. 22 Aug. 1986: 76-77.

Smith, Paul. *Discerning the Subject*. Minneapolis: U of Minnesota P, 1988.

Smith, Russell. "The Right to Cry Woolf in a CanLit Review." *Globe and Mail* 16 Apr. 1994: C5.

Smith, Sidonie. *A Poetics of Women's Autobiography*. Bloomington: Indiana UP, 1987.

Spender, Dale. *Man Made Language*. 2nd ed. London: Routledge and Kegan Paul, 1985.

Stainsby, Mari. "Alice Munro Talks With Mari Stainsby." *British Columbia Library Quarterly* 35.1 (July 1971): 27-30.

Steele, Apollonia. Personal Interview. October 1996.

Steele, Charles, ed. *Taking Stock: The Calgary Conference on the Canadian Novel*. Downsview, ON: ECW Press, 1982.

Stewart, Sandy. *From Coast to Coast: A Personal History of Radio in Canada*. Rev. Toronto: CBC Enterprises, 1985.

Struthers, J.R. (Tim). "Alice Munro and the American South." *The Canadian Novel: A Critical Anthology*. Vol. 1: *Here and Now*. Ed. John Moss. Toronto: NC Press, 1978. 121-33. Original quote from Mari Stainsby.

———. "The Real Material: An Interview with Alice Munro." MacKendrick. 5-38.

Tausky, Thomas. "Biocritical Essay." *The Alice Munro Papers: First Accession*. Calgary: U of Calgary P, 1986. ix-xxiv.

Thacker, Robert. "Alice Munro: An Annotated Bibliography." *The Annotated Bibliography of Canada's Major Authors*. Ed. Jack David. Downsview, ON: ECW Press, 1984. 354-414.

———. "'Clear Jelly': Alice Munro's Narrative Dialectics." MacKendrick. 37-60.

Thomas, Audrey. "Initram." *Ladies and Escorts.* Ottawa: Oberon P, 1977. 88-107.

Thomas, Clara. "Myth and Manitoba in *The Diviners.*" *The Canadian Novel Here and Now.* Ed. John Moss. 103-18.

Thompson, Kent. "The Canadian Short Story in English and the Little Magazines—1971." *World Literature Written in English* 11 (April 1972): 15-24.

Thorpe, James. *Principles of Textual Criticism.* San Marino, CA: Huntington Library, 1972.

Tomashevsky, Boris. "Literature and Biography." Burke 81-89.

Twersky Reimer, Gail. "Revisions of Labor in Margaret Oliphant's Autobiography." *Life Lines: Theorizing Women's Autobiography.* Ed. Bella Brodzki and Celeste Schenck. Ithaca, NY: Cornell UP, 1988. 203-20.

Twigg, Alan. *Vancouver and Its Writers.* Madeira Park, BC: Harbour, 1986.

———. "What Is." *For Openers: Conversations with 24 Canadian Writers.* Madeira Park, BC: Harbour, 1981. 13-20.

Wachtel, Eleanor. "Alice Munro." *Writers and Company.* Toronto: Knopf, 1993. 101-12.

Wainwright, J.A., ed. *A Very Large Soul: Selected Letters from Margaret Laurence to Canadian Writers.* Dunvegan, ON: Cormorant Press, 1995.

Ward, Olivia. "Men Are Suffering Too." *The Toronto Star* 6 May 1979: D6.

Wayne, Joyce. "Huron County Blues." *Books in Canada* Oct. 1982: 9-12.

Weaver, Robert. Introduction. *The* Anthology *Anthology: A Selection from 30 Years of CBC Radio's* Anthology. Ed. Robert Weaver. Toronto: Macmillan, 1984. xii-xiii.

———. Introduction. *Canadian Short Stories.* Ed. Robert Weaver. Toronto: Oxford UP, 1960. ix-xiii.

———. Preface. *Canadian Short Stories.* 5th Series. Ed. Robert Weaver. Toronto: Oxford UP, 1991. ix-xii.

Weaver, Robert, and William Toye, eds. *The Oxford Anthology of Canadian Literature.* Toronto: Oxford UP, 1973.

———. eds. *The Oxford Anthology of Canadian Literature.* 2nd ed. Toronto: Oxford UP, 1981.

Weedon, Chris. *Feminist Practice and Poststructuralist Theory.* Oxford: Basil Blackwell, 1987.

Weir, E. Austin. *The Struggle for National Broadcasting in Canada.* Toronto: McClelland and Stewart, 1965.

Wernick, Andrew. "Authorship and the Supplement of Promotion." Biriotti 85-102.

West, James L. III. *American Authors and the Literary Marketplace Since 1900.* Philadelphia: U of Philadelphia P, 1988.

Williams, Raymond. *Keywords: A Vocabulary of Culture.* Rev. ed. London: Fontana, 1989.

"Writers' Writers." *Books in Canada* Jan.-Feb. 1987: 8-11.

"Writing's Something I Did Like the Ironing." *Globe and Mail* 11 Dec. 1982: E1.

# INDEX

academic canonization, 147, 151
academic critics, 137
academic reader, 22
academy, 111, 135-36, 138-39, 142
"active but not sovereign protagonist," 66, 116. *See also* Weedon
Adachi, Ken, 37
aesthetic, 128, 129, 132, 145-46
aestheticism, 152
Alfred A. Knopf, 8, 18, 75-76, 107. *See also* Close, Ann
Alice Munro fonds, 13
Althusser, Louis, 63, 65
*Anthology*, 26, 31, 34, 54-55
Appleton Century Crofts, 46
artist as product, producer, citizen, 114-17, 125, 139, 142
Atwood, Margaret, 39, 40, 115, 123, 125, 150, 153, 154-55; and cultural nationalism, 36, 38
author, 138; and agent relationship, 70; as creator, 150; definition of, 150; "godlike," 144; literary, 21, 117; "recip-

ient of the Muse's bounty," 124; regional, 114
author function, 4-5, 7, 17, 31, 68, 72, 99, 122; in copyright law, 5; and "plurality of selves," 10, 16, 41, 110, 138
authoritative text, 109
authorship, 3-4; and autonomy, 33, 49, 86, 146; construct of literary, 84; contemporary theories of, 9, 115; cultural demands of, 146; and gender, 64-65, 67-69, 75, 122, 144; and genre, 65, 81; myths of, 31, 49; popular vs. serious, 88, 134; sociocultural ideologies of, 151
autobiographical, 114, 124, 126-27, 145
autobiography, 3, 122-24, 127, 138

Bader, A. L., 87, 120
Banting, Pamela, 15
Barber Agency, the, 61, 70
Barber, Virginia, ix, xv, 8, 13, 19, 21, 48, 59, 70, 101, 111, 122,